From Poverty
TO THE
PROMISE

Shanika A. Stewart

Published By: TJW Enterprises, LLC.

Purpose

This book has been inspired to help others share their stories. To give others hope who may be experiencing poverty in any way. This book is to activate one's faith and hope in the Lord that His promises may be fulfilled in their lives. This is a reminder for readers that they can come out of any situation or any hardships through the spoken word of God so that God's promises for their lives can be fulfilled. Readers will know that the curse of poverty can be broken and destroyed off the lives of God's people through his word so I hope that these stories bless your life and encourage you in more ways than one through the lives of every Co-Author as they share their stories.

Introduction

As you journey through this book may the stories you read give you hope and inspire you to trust the promises of God concerning your life. This book is purposed to give hope to the hopeless and to possibly change one's perspective on how they view God and His Word. The stories that you read are testimonies on how God took the authors from *Poverty into His Promises*.

Foreword
by Dr. Kishma George

From Poverty to the Promise-Stories of Victory was compiled by Dr. Shanika Stewart, a dreamer, and a world changer on the rise. This book is a collection of amazing co-authors who wished to help others by sharing their powerful overcoming stories and testimonies. The stories and testimonies will activate one's faith and hope in the Lord!

It is hoped that after reading, From Poverty to the Promise - Stories of Victory, the readers will gain confidence and be inspired to feel that they can come out of any situation or hardship through the spoken Word of God. May this book change one's perspective to a positive outcome! Be empowered to CHANGE with the help of God!

Dr. Kishma A. George

Table of Contents

*Your words will create
your future!*

PROPHETESS SHANIKA STEWART

Prophetess Shanika Ann Stewart is a wife a mother and the business owner of:

Anointed Touch Barber and Beauty &
Anointed Touch Apparel
T.H.R.I.V.E Counseling Solutions LLC

CHAPTER 1

Don't Be Distracted Your Time is Now

When poverty speaks you must know how to speak back with authority and total confidence in what God has promised you. Poverty has a voice and it sounds like, "I can't, I don't have enough, or I need, need, need". Poverty is not your friend and poverty is not a promise from God, it's a state of mind that none of us need to be in, but many of us find ourselves there knowingly or unknowingly. I believe we all have experienced poverty in one way or another. When you define the word poverty, based on the dictionary.com website, it means **the state of being extremely poor**. That can be mentally, financially, physically, and spiritually. Another definition is the state of being poor; insufficient in need, in want, hardship, lack, impoverished or ignorance.

When we understand the purpose of the Lord's mission here on earth it is, I believe, to restore mankind back to our rightful place in the Kingdom of God. The first Adam fell into sin and caused hardship, suffering and pain to come upon us, but the second Adam which was Jesus Christ came to restore us back into sonship with our Heavenly Father, to break the bands of wickedness off our life, and to fulfill the promises of God. I believe with the help of Christ and His obedience, our life became better, and we no longer have to struggle, but now prosper, and thrive in the kingdom of God. We now have dominion and rule in the earth to fulfill God's original plan for our lives as sons of God. Poverty keeps you stuck, and it doesn't allow you to live your life to the fullest. I experienced poverty growing up as a young girl where I had to settle for hand-me-down clothes. I wasn't very educated, and I wasn't able to do a lot of things or go to many places because of the lack of funds or resources.

I was raised in the projects and my mom did the best she could to take care of me and my two brothers. Life was a bit rough, but I had hopes and dreams to hold on to. I was a dreamer at a young age with big dreams. At a young age I learned how to pray and although I didn't understand the Bible in its entirety I would always hold on to Psalms 23 verses 1-6 KJV, **"The Lord is my shepherd; I shall not want. He maketh me lie down in green pastures: he leadeth me beside the still waters. He restoreth my soul: he leadeth me in the paths of righteousness for his name sake. Yea though I walk through the valley of the shadow of death, I will fear no evil: for thou art with; me thy rod and thy staff they comfort me. Thou preparest a table before me in the presence of mine enemies: thou anointest my head with oil; my cup runneth over. Surely goodness and mercy shall follow me all the days of my life: and I will dwell in the house of the Lord forever. Amen."** That prayer literally kept me during some of the most challenging times of my life growing up. I eventually began to meet some amazing people who God allowed me to meet that introduced me to the kingdom of God and His promises. They accepted me where I was and helped me grow by the grace of God. I had to learn from some mistakes I made, and I just want to share a few nuggets with you that helped me get through to overcome poverty and experience the promises of God.

These are a few scriptures that help me to understand that I didn't have to envy anyone or do bad things to receive God's promises. I simply had to seek Him first and His way of doing things and whatever I needed would be added unto me. According to Matthew 6:33 KJV sometimes we can get anxious before our time when there's a time and season for everything and sometimes the Lord has to do a work for us and work on us so that He may be able to work through us so His promises may be fulfilled in our lives.

THE BIBLE SAYS:

Proverbs 23:17-18 KJV
> *"Let not thine heart envy sinners: But be thou in the fear of the LORD all the day long. For surely there is an end; And thine expectation shall not be cut off."*

Envy - Desire to have a quality, possession, or other desirable attribute belonging to (someone else). Verb

Surely - 1. Used to emphasize without doubt; certain.

End - A final part of something, especially a period of time, an activity, or a story.

Expectation - A strong belief that something will happen or be the case in the future. It's a belief that someone will or should achieve something.

Proverbs 23:17-18 MSG

"Don't for a minute, envy careless rebels; soak yourself in the Fear-of- GOD — That's where your future lies. Then you won't be left with an armload of nothing."

Proverbs 23:17-18 ERV

"Never envy evil people, but always respect the Lord. This will give you something to hope for that will not disappoint you."

Isaiah 55:6-13 KJV

"Seek ye the LORD while he may be found, call ye upon him while he is near: let the wicked forsake his way, and the unrighteous man his thoughts: and let him return unto the LORD, and he will have mercy upon him; and to our God, for he will abundantly pardon. For my thoughts are not your thoughts, neither are your ways my ways, saith the LORD. For as the heavens are higher than the earth, so are my ways higher than your ways, and my thoughts than your thoughts. For as the rain cometh down, and the snow from heaven, and returneth not thither, but watereth the earth, and maketh it bring forth and bud, that it may give seed to the sower, and bread to the eater: so shall my word be that goeth forth out of my mouth: it shall not return unto me void, but it shall accomplish that which I please, and it shall prosper in the thing whereto I sent it. For ye shall go out with joy and be led forth with peace: the mountains and the hills shall break forth before you into singing, and all the trees of the field shall clap their hands. Instead of

the thorn shall come up the fir tree, and instead of the brier shall come up the myrtle tree: and it shall be to the LORD for a name, for an everlasting sign that shall not be cut off."

Psalm 23:1-6 ESV

"The Lord is my shepherd; I shall not want. He makes me lie down in green pastures. He leads me beside still waters. He restores my soul. He leads me in paths of righteousness for his name's sake. Even though I walk through the valley of the shadow of death, I will fear no evil, for you are with me; your rod and your staff, they comfort me. You prepare a table before me in the presence of my enemies; you anoint my head with oil; my cup overflows. Surely goodness and mercy shall follow me all the days of my life, and I shall dwell in the house of the Lord forever."

So while you are believing God for his promises, remember God's promises are **YES** and **AMEN**. He said above all He wishes that we would prosper and be in good health even as our soul prospers (3 John 2 KJV). I believe the benefits that God has given us are His promises. We can confidently hold on to all He promised to give us. That includes healing, deliverance, peace, strength, courage, joy, faith, hope, love, wealth, health, wholeness and so much more. We must always remember our words have power, and life and death are in the power of our tongue, those that love it will eat the fruit thereof. (Proverbs 18:21 KJV). Always remember to affirm and encourage yourself in the Lord.

AFFIRMATIONS

Affirmation - It's the action or process of affirming something or being affirmed. Also, it's emotional support or encouragement

Reciting affirmations is one way to speak life into your situation. It is also how you can encourage yourself and speak life into your situation. Here are some keywords to help us understand how powerful affirmations really are and describe what we are actually doing when we affirm ourselves.

- We Make a Declaration - the formal announcement of the beginning of a state or condition
- We Make a Statement - a definite or clear expression of something in speech or writing
- We Make a Proclamation - a clear declaration of something
- We Have Assurance - a positive declaration intended to give confidence, a promise
- We Make a Vow - a solemn promise and come in agreement with the Word of The Lord
- Confirmation - the action of confirming something or the state of being confirmed
- Endorsement - an act of giving one's public approval or support to someone or something
- We Make An Agreement:
    - We agree with what God has promised us so an Oath is a solemn promise, often invoking a divine witness, regarding one's future action or behavior
    - We agree with what God's Promise declaration or assurance that one will do a particular thing or that a particular thing will happen

MY GIFT TO YOU

My Gift To You - Affirmation nuggets you may use daily to encourage yourself. I would encourage you to recite or declare these daily or create your own so that you may be empowered to endure the process of going from <u>Poverty to The Promise of God</u>. You shall have whatever you say. **Your words have power** so speak well over your life and watch your words work in your favor.

Here are some affirmations I would like to leave you with:

- Bro/Sis you are Loved
- Bro/ Sis you are Beautiful
- Bro/ Sis you are Smart
- Bro/Sis you are Wise
- Bro/Sis you are Intelligent
- Bro/Sis you are Healed
- Bro/ Sis you are Whole
- Bro/Sis you are Healthy
- Bro/Sis you are Wealthy
- Bro/Sis you are Debt Free
- Bro/Sis you are Blessed
- Bro/Sis you are More Than Enough
- Bro/Sis you are The One God Chose
- Bro/Sis you are Strong
- Bro/Sis you are Fearless
- Bro/Sis you are Faithful
- Bro/Sis you are Courageous
- Bro/Sis you are Protected

- Bro/Sis you are Thriving
- Bro/Sis you are still Standing
- Bro/Sis you are a Wealth Magnet
- Bro/Sis you are Favored by God
- Bro/Sis you are Fearfully and Wonderfully Made
- Bro/Sis you are a Great Mother/Father
- Bro/Sis you are a Great Wife/Husband
- Bro/Sis you are a Woman or Man of God
- Bro/Sis you are a Proverb 31 Woman/Mighty Man of Valor
- Bro/Sis you are a Prophet of God
- Bro/Sis you are a Worshiper
- Bro/Sis you are a Warrior
- Bro/Sis you are an Intercessor
- Bro/Sis you are a Daughter/Son of The King
- Bro/Sis you are a Boss
- Bro/Sis you are an Entrepreneur
- Bro/Sis you are a Kingdom Underwriter
- Bro/Sis you are a Seed Sower
- Bro/Sis you are a Giver
- Bro/Sis you are Friend of God
- Bro/Sis you are here on purpose for God's purpose
- Bro/Sis you are Graced by God
- Bro/Sis you are a great Sister/Brother
- Bro/Sis you are a great Daughter/son
- Bro/Sis you are a great Listener
- Bro/Sis you are a great Leader
- Bro/Sis you are a great Person

ANTHONY STEWART

In 2010, Anthony Stewart started pastoring and birthed a ministry called Active Faith Christian Center, teaching, and preaching faith and prosperity. He learned that when working the principles of God the Lord will truly bless you.
He is a Millionaire in the making.

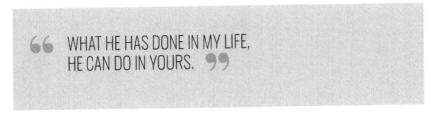

WHAT HE HAS DONE IN MY LIFE, HE CAN DO IN YOURS.

CHAPTER 2

From Poverty to Prosperity

As a young boy born in the mid sixties I think just about everyone was impoverished, but as children we didn't know it. We didn't know what wealth was and we always had the things we needed coming up. I can remember my mom working for ten dollars a day and she walked three miles to work. Coming up I found out that I had a gift of fixing and creating things, because we really didn't have money to replace anything that was broken. I created a lot of things with my hands.

My parents purchased a Jim Walter home that cost $3,000 took them about 2 decades for them to pay for it. I remember the note being $63 a month which was a struggle. After my parents died years later, we ended up renting the house for a few years. A storm hit later and the house sat up for about five years, holes in the roof, and holes in the floors. My brothers and I discussed tearing it down and I heard the Lord saying that this is your inheritance. Within a year I totally restored the house in honor of my parents.

Right after high school I attended college for two years. I was driving a 1969 Ford Galaxy at the time; and remember my mother scrapping up three dollars in change for gas money. I thought to myself, I can't do this anymore, I need to find a job. A couple of years after quitting college I couldn't even find a good paying job. There's an English Proverb that says, "an idle mind is the devil's workshop". I was introduced to selling drugs. I was trying to come out of poverty the best way I knew how, but the Bible declares in Proverbs 14:12 KJV that, *"there is a way that seems right unto man, but the end thereof is destruction."* I was making money, but I was not prospering. I had no peace in my life. I was in and out of jail but in 1994 I ended up giving my life to Jesus, and my life hasn't ever been the same. When I found out about Faith in God, the Promises of God and working the Principles of God, I went from poverty to prosperity.

I realized that He blesses the works of your hand. In 2010, I started pastoring and birthed a ministry called Active Faith Christian Center, teaching, and preaching faith and prosperity. I've learned that when working the principles of God the Lord will truly bless you. I want to encourage those who are reading this book that God can truly bless you if your faith is active in Him. I am a Millionaire in the making. God has brought me from poverty to prosperity so be encouraged because He is not a respecter of person. What He has done in my life, He can do in yours.

JOHN KUN KUN

- Bishop John Kun Kun is the Senior Pastor of the City of Light Church of God Barnersville Estate in Monrovia, Liberia since 1998.
- Former Administrative Bishop and Missionary of Church of God in Sierra Leone and Republic of Guinea from 2006-2010 and the Republic of Mali from 2010-2014
- Former President of the Liberia Fellowship of Full Gospel Ministers and Churches in Liberia 2014-2021
- 2nd Vice President Haven of Rest Ministers Network with headquarters in South Africa, International Coordinator Jesus Global Harvest Ministries with headquarters in Abuja, Nigeria.

Website: www.johnkunkun.org
YouTube Bishop John Kun Kun
Facebook John Kun Kun
Email: johnkkun68@gmail.com
Whatsapp +231777022774/+231886551252/

"God can take you from the place of poverty and bring you to the place of promise by His word."

CHAPTER 3

The Hidden Story of My Glory

I am John Kun Kun. I was born to the union of Charles T. Kun and Esther D. Kun in the year 1968, April 25th, in Monrovia, Liberia. My parents hail from Grand Kru County, one of the fifteen counties southeast of Liberia. I am the first of seventeen children that my father has, and eight of them by my mother, his wife. I grew up in Douala, Mombo town, one of the least developed areas in Liberia and is considered one of the hostile communities. I grew up in Douala and Mombo town communities, which are situated in the Bushrod Island, Liberia around Monrovia. There I received my primary and high school education from St. Mary Catholic High School in 1986.

In 1970, at the age of two, my parents gave me to my aunt who began taking care of my welfare until I graduated from high school. My aunt was a seamstress, making not less than 3 dollars USD per suit; we survived with that amount for feeding, schooling, and clothing (1970-1986). At the shop where my aunt worked, I was responsible for pressing clothes. During my high school days, I earned a scholarship from the then president of the Republic of Liberia (Samuel K. Doe) primarily because of academic excellence. The Catholic Church of Liberia also awarded me a scholarship because they wanted me to become a priest and serve the Catholic Church.

At the age of 21, during the outbreak of the Civil War, 1989, I became the bread winner of my family because my parents became incapacitated; in that same year my aunt's (Elizabeth Wolo) husband died in June.

During the Civil War 1990, I ran from Douala to Bardnersville to seek refuge. When the Civil War subsided because of ongoing peace talks at the time, I got on my feet knowing I was responsible for my siblings that were with me, and my parents and other siblings that were elsewhere. During these times I found a house that was abandoned because the owner of the house fled the war; so we moved in and started living there. After the Civil War had subsided, I started working as a voluntary worker with some NGO organizations by doing distribution of food in the communities, through which I also received something for sustenance for my family and myself.

In the year 1994 that process stopped and I started teaching at various schools to earn a living. I conducted Bible classes with several schools as a way of evangelism, to name a few: E. Jonathan Goodridge High School, Jimmy Jolocon High School, Konawa High School and many other schools that catered to the needs of my siblings. Meanwhile, I had no foundation of wealth, and neither was there anyone financially potent in my family. I did not know anyone in the family who had ever built a house or ever drove their own car. We were not poor because of the war but were already financially impotent, which was worse. During the period of the Civil War, we had no one to turn to for help except God's divine intervention. The death of my Aunt Elizabeth's husband and the inception of the Civil War affected my college education, which made me drop out. Our parents went through a lot of struggles to see us through high school, however I had divine intervention. Imagine what it is like for a father without income to educate and feed 17 children in a country without welfare programs and health insurance.

I was born again August 5, 1990, and this changed my entire life, mindset, and destiny. Even when I was persecuted for the Gospel, it did not turn me back to the life I used to live or give up on the promises of God. In the year 1994, I was a member of a ministry called Soul Winning Evangelistic Ministry. During these times I would walk from Bardnersville to Monrovia to preach and sometimes to listen to the word of God. The distance we would cover while walking took about 2 hours. I had only one pair of shoes and a pair of jeans at the time. Many days I would sleep hungry because there was no money to buy food, for I never had anything. I would preach from place to place and go home and sleep hungry. I was born again in the City of Light Church of God. There I started ministry by cleaning the church, cutting grass, and taking care of the bathroom, evangelizing, and teaching in the church. I worked in the church for two years,doing every aspect of ministry before the Pastor of the church appeared from where he was displaced because of the Civil War. The pastor then decided to pay me $50 Liberian dollars (LD) per month, which was at that time (1992) the equivalent of USD $1.50. I was never paid from 1992 until I became the assistant Pastor of the Church and then I began to get the allowance of $50.00 LD per month, which was my salary when I got married July 26, 1996. That amount remained my salary until June 1998, when I became the Senior Pastor of the City of Light Church of God. As a man that was involved with evangelism, I brought many people to the church. When they gave testimonies and mentioned my name, the pastor got angry and drove me out of the church. I went to another church of God to work. I had to walk almost every day with or without food to eat. I was glad that I had the right atmosphere to operate and carry on with ministry. The distance I walked many days for ministry took one hour fifteen minutes to the church, and one hour fifteen minutes back home daily.

I was evicted from many houses I lived in because of the preaching of the Gospel and was taken to prison on four occasions. I faced persecution because the youth were being transformed because of the Gospel that was preached to them by me. During that time girls were involved with sex trade to feed their families and for survival. We began to teach them how to live by faith, which their parents rejected. That provoked them to persecute and incarcerate me at the major prison center, South Beach Prison in Monrovia, Liberia.

In the midst of all that was happening, the lady that finally became my wife prophesied to me in an all-night prayer tarry. She prophesied that the Lord was going to bless my ministry with signs and wonders, miracles, greater power, and grace, and that the Lord would cause me to travel around the world preaching the Gospel with FAVOUR. I did not believe anything she said at that time because my team and I had just walked two and half hours (and were heavily perspiring) because we had no money for transportation. But God is faithful even when we are not faithful, and He has brought it to pass today.

When I wanted to marry my wife, I had two pairs of jeans, a few shirts and T-shirts, and just one pair of brown boots that a friend gave me from the USA. My wife's parents and sisters said I was too poor to be her husband. They preferred a guy (who was not born again) from the UK to be her husband instead of a Holy Ghost-filled man like me. Thank God she fasted and prayed, and the Lord revealed me as her husband. When I wrote to my wife's father and met with him, he asked me to buy him two pairs of boots because he loved boots. Meanwhile, I didn't even have shoes for myself to wear on the wedding day because I could not afford it. I borrowed the shoes of my spiritual son to wear for the wedding. After the wedding, I returned the shoes; when my wife started to ask for the beautiful shoes that I used for the wedding I had no answer. I pretended not to hear her. Finally, I told her they were my spiritual son's shoes. This was one of the ways poverty had disgraced me in life, and now today, by the grace of God, I have many shoes and can afford many more expensive shoes. My wife's family were not involved in the wedding and never attended the ceremony. However, it was good and went well. Although we did not have a car to drive us to the church for the wedding, we managed to get the bride to the church with someone's car, while my men and I walked to the church. The truth is, I was very poor and did not look like I had a future.

When we got married, we had over 17 people living with us and we could not afford to provide food. Let me announce to you that the promise is greater than the problems and challenges. My wife had to learn tie-dye and sold used clothes for our feeding. She also learned sewing and became a seamstress. There was a time that the landlord asked us to leave his house and we had nowhere to go. Our children and I went to squat with a lady in her house, while my wife was also squatting with a sister from the church's praise team. Whenever the lady I stayed with went out of town, my wife would move with me, and we stayed in the women's room. Whenever she returned home my wife and I would separate until she would leave again for another trip.

In July 1998 we went to church on a Sunday and were drenched by the rain. When we got to the church, an old woman suggested that the church should raise offerings and buy us an umbrella which caused $2.00 USD at that time. I came up by faith and said, "Thanks for your concern, but the Lord wants to give me a car and not an umbrella." The people laughed because the CHURCH at that time did not have the capacity to buy me a car. By the grace of the almighty God, four weeks after I sowed into the buying of another Pastor's car, a sister in the church gifted me with my first car in the same July that I spoke it.

It was a difficult time. Many days we had no food to eat and we went to bed hungry. I thought, "You're married to a girl, and you can't afford food and clothes for her." It wasn't easy, but we trusted the Lord. While sitting at home hungry, God would lead someone to our house with food. They would say that the soul winning group decided to fast for 52 days to win him over to the Lord, but everybody declined except me. When I went to meet him it was terrifying. By the grace of God, he got saved. After he turned his weapon in, he never had a place to live. He came over to my house with 15 other fighters. My wife had to sell more items to feed all those people; it was a very difficult time. Sister Ling Nelson gave us the house, which only had two rooms. Fifteen persons were staying in one room, and my wife and I were in another room and we had to accommodate two other persons in our room.

As a result of all that I suffered, and considering my family background, I reflected on my experiences that led me to taking spiritual actions. This included a time of fasting and doing all night prayers for a month. Then I realized that there was a demonic covenant causing poverty in the family. There also was a wrong mindset within the family that we were not qualified to own good things, get better positions, obtain higher education, or prosper in life. So, after deep reflection on this, I moved into fasting and prayer to break the curse of poverty. *I also made a decision to search in the word of God for covenant prosperity principles and get hold of scriptures that would change my way of thinking from negative mindset to positive kingdom mindset.* This helped me to know that I was never too poor to help another person. No matter my position or condition, there is someone that I can always help which will provoke divine help in my life. So, that was how I became a covenant giver since 1998 -- by giving tithes of 25% and good offerings.

Secondly, I started looking out for people who had greater needs than mine; I had to use my little resources that couldn't solve my problems to meet their needs. For example, my wife and I had to move to a new place from where we were. We needed $24,000 Liberian dollars, which is equivalent to $350 USD, but then a friend of mine gave us $15,000 LD which is equivalent to $200 USD. Then one of our spiritual sons also had a need of rental fees and his rent was $3600 LD and we helped him meet his need. Afterward, our church overseer at the time blessed us with $12,000 LD equivalent to $160 USD, and we were able to complete our rent for relocation. Because that worked, it became one of our secrets to prosperity. *This helped me understand that it is not enough to only break the curse of poverty, but there must be an application of sowing and reaping principles.* When curses are broken, and there is no sowing of seed, there will be no reaping of harvest. From 1998, when I took over the ministry with fifteen adults and about twenty children, God began to bless and increase the church numerically, financially, and spiritually with salvation, healing, and miracles. The church grew from thirty-five to over one thousand in membership, having potential members with key positions in national government, business setting and other corporations.

Today our church also produces graduates from many universities in and out of Liberia. I came from place of being a cleaner in my local church in 1990 to become an ordained Bishop of the Church of God World Missions Liberia (April 2006) with assignments as overseer to the Republic of Sierra Leone, and the Republic of Guinea, (2006-2010), and overseer to the Republic of Mali (2010-2014). Since 1996 to this time, I have traveled extensively throughout the continent of Africa, namely: Nigeria, Ivory Coast, South Africa, Kenya, Tanzania, Ethiopia, Burundi, Ghana, Sierra Leone, Burkina Faso, Mali, Togo, Benin, and many others. By the special grace of God, I have traveled to the USA over 22 times since 2007. I have also traveled to Europe, to name a few in Europe: UK, Belgium, France, Australia, Asia, China and South Korea and many states in America including Hawaii Islands, Central and South America, Dominican Republic, and the Bahamas. I am preaching and teaching the gospel as was prophesied by my wife that God had promised to take me to the Nations.

By the grace of God I, who couldn't afford rent, am now living in my own house and own a two-story, four-apartment building. I have owned several vehicles and have given away about eight (8) cars. I have also built a three-bedroom house for my parents. I have served in several capacities of leadership in the body of Christ in Liberia, Nigeria, South Africa, and as Ambassador of Resurrection Life Ministries with headquarters in Canada. I am serving on several humanitarian and institutional boards. God can take you from the place of poverty and bring you to the place of promise by His word.

"Now I commit you to God and to the word of His grace which is able to build you up and to give you an inheritance amongst all who are sanctified".
(Acts 20:32)

Bishop John Kun Kun is the international speaker of the Africa transformation conferences around Africa. He was made the Ambassador to the nations for the Resurrection Life Ministries on August 30,2020 with headquarters in Canada as a revival, crusade, radio and television speaker. He ministers at many places around the world including Africa, Europe, Australia, USA, China, South Korea, Central America, etc. He also serves on several boards of institutions and humanitarian organizations. The anointing and power of God for signs and wonders, healings, deliverance, and transformation of lives are always present when the word of God is preached and taught by him. Many men and women from ghettos, demonic backgrounds, criminal backgrounds, including warlords in Liberia like the notorious former general butt naked who is now Evangelist Joshua Milton Blahyi. He is the author of the book 'Recovery from Spiritual Bondage.' He is married to Prophetess, Pastor Yvonne Kun and blessed with three beautiful daughters, several grandchildren, and many spiritual children around the world, making great impact. To God be the glory.

TARSHA N. HOWARD

Tarsha N. Howard, MPA

Tarsha Howard is a native resident of Brooklyn, New York is a loving mom and enjoys guiding her son Joshua on the path of life. He is a born again Christian and applies Biblical principles to solve real-life problems. In her church cover, she is a Prophetess with a burden to pray for others, she is also a prophetic intercessor. God has given her a mandate to pray for those called to the marketplace as well as teach marketplace ministry. In the marketplace, Tarsha is a Certified Legal Support Professional. As a part time Kingdom Entrepreneur, Tarsha formulates organic beauty care products. She owns Elohim Beauty, LLC and PrettyOrganix, LLC based in Brooklyn, New York.

Instagram: @TarshaGlobal
Instagram: @marketplacechamber
Website: www.elohimbeauty.com

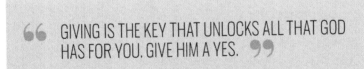

66 GIVING IS THE KEY THAT UNLOCKS ALL THAT GOD HAS FOR YOU. GIVE HIM A YES. 99

CHAPTER 4

The Supernatural Realm of Giving

"Give, and it shall be given unto you; good measure, pressed down, and shaken together, and running over, shall men give into your bosom. For with the same measure that ye mete withal it shall be measured to you again." **(Luke 6:38 KJV)**

There is a law of finance in God's Kingdom. God's financial laws are not of this world. In the Kingdom, there are a set of supernatural laws that are created and designed for His children to prosper regardless of the world's circumstances. Over the course of time, the children of darkness have adopted these same principles in order to move ahead and amass great wealth. The word of God says, *"the children of darkness are wiser than the children of light"* according to Luke 16:8. Amid gaining wealth, the children of darkness never credit their prosperity principles to the Kingdom of God. Satan was the highest archangel. He dwelled in the Kingdom of God until he wanted to be like God (Isaiah 14:14). Pride took a hold of Satan, and he was cast out of heaven with one third of the Angels. What does this mean? It means that Satan is the greatest imitator of God. He will continue to use the very strategies that he learned while he was in heaven to train his army to advance in the earth realm.

Now that we have a foundation of how the kingdom of darkness used kingdom principles to gain prosperity, let us decipher where the children of light missed the mark. When I came to the Lord back in 2000, I was very ecstatic. I was happy to get to know the Lord and all that was in store for me. I had a nice career at a law firm and my life as a young woman blossomed. I began to travel and explore the world as well. God began to move me from one church to another so I could gain more knowledge of His word. The new church was unlike the church where I got saved. The new church was a holiness church. The women did not wear pants, or make-up and holiness was taught as a way of life. One thing stood out to me; it was deemed holy to be in poverty. In the same tone, the church stressed to give your tithe. In my opinion, it was also contradictory because the tithe opens the door for prosperity. God has not required poverty to be a sign of "holiness" unto him. The word of God says that God has an abundant life available to us all. *"The thief cometh not but to steal and to kill and to destroy. I come that they might have life, and that they might have it more abundantly."* (John 10:10 KJV)

The enemy stole the identity of the church by creating a doctrine that taught poverty is the best way to serve God. How can the gospel move forth in the earth realm without finances? As I moved forward, God began to teach me the basic principles of "God's Financial Kingdom." For a season, God removed me from the church system. I was still born again but I could not stay under the teaching that if I lived in poverty, I am pleasing God.

During this time, I also had financial struggles. One day, I had a dream. I fell asleep and the Lord showed me a barn full of wheat. A large hand came down and took a small portion from the large pile. The large hand came to my face to show me how small of a portion was taken and there was a large amount in the barn still left over. I woke up and a voice told me to start tithing and to sow seeds. There is only one place in the bible that God asks us to test him, it is in Malachi 3:10-11:

"Bring ye all the tithes into the storehouse, that there may be meat in mine house, and prove me now herewith, saith the Lord of hosts, if I will not open you the windows of heaven, and pour you out a blessing, that there shall not be room enough to receive it. And I will rebuke the devourer for your sakes, and he shall not destroy the fruits of your ground; neither shall your vine cast her fruit before the time in the field, saith the Lord of hosts."
(Malachi 3:10-11 KJV)

I was not a committed tither in the former church. I would give sporadically. It was not in my heart to give consistently. I would still receive blessings, but they too were sporadic. I gave an offering at every Sunday service, but my tithe was not consistent. Since I was not in a church at the time, I decided to locate a ministry online to start my consistent tithing. Once I found a ministry, I decided to tithe every time I would get paid. There were new and exciting things that began to happen to me. One astonishing thing I noticed, I never had to look for a job. The jobs supernaturally found me. I also would get positions that came with an uncommon high salary. People would ask me how I am able to travel and have a good life as a single mom. I live in New York and the cost of living is high. I travel at least six times a year with my son to beautiful destinations. People always want to know my secret. My secret is, I am a giver.

Currently, I consistently tithe and sow financial seeds to my church covering. I also give financial seeds to other ministries where I am a partner. There is a supernatural dimension that you will live in once you make the decision to become a **"Kingdom Financier."** What is a Kingdom Financier? **It is a person who has dedicated his or her life to underwrite Kingdom initiatives.** Once you decide to live this lifestyle, God will cause you to live a life that has uncommon supernatural provision, opportunity and open doors of favor. It is also spiritual law:

> *"While the earth remaineth, seedtime and harvest, and cold and heat, summer and winter, and day and night shall not cease."* **(Genesis 8:22 KJV)**

The promise in God's word is there will be seedtime (giving) and harvest (receiving). *"God's word shall not return void, it will accomplish what it was sent out to do"* (Isaiah 55:11 KJV). Imagine living a life of more than enough. That life is possible once you become a consistent giver. God also promised that he would open the windows of heaven and pour you so many blessings that you will not have room enough to receive (Malachi 3:10 KJV). What are those windows? They are heavenly portals that open over your mind to give you ideas on how to create wealth, divine direction and supernatural strategies to overcome your current financial circumstances. Have you ever had a "God inspired idea?" If not, when you become a consistent giver, you will have God inspired ideas on a regular basis. You will begin to live in an **"Open Heaven."** Your mind will begin to generate money making ideas to take you from poverty into prosperity.

If you desire to live in the Supernatural Realm of Giving, become a Kingdom Financier. You can start from where you are. God just wants a yes. When you take care of God's Kingdom, he will take care of you. You shall lack nothing. You will begin to see all our heart's desires being fulfilled. As you support Kingdom initiatives, you will have all things added unto you. God is looking for faithful people who will make the commitment to give and support ministries that are on the front lines. This remnant will need faithful financial supporters who have a heart to finance God's kingdom without wavering. There is a great reward to those who answer the call.

> *But seek ye first the kingdom of God, and his righteousness; and all these things shall be added unto you.* **(Matthew 6:33 KJV)**

I answered the call. Since that time, I have had a rewarding career, became an author and I am a part time Kingdomprenuer. A **Kingdomprenuer** is a <u>person who is a part of God's Kingdom and becomes an entrepreneur to glorify God</u>. When God leads, I will transition to become a full time Kingdomprenuer so I can underwrite kingdom initiatives and advance God's agenda in the earth realm. Giving is the key that unlocks all that God has for you. Give him a yes.

MIKE EBRON

Michael Ebron has been graced with the ability to travel and minister the word of the Lord. He serves as a personal intercessor to elite celebrities in the Gospel industry. He is also a national recording artist with a prayer album, author, veteran, kingdom entrepreneur building an entire network of kingdom believers, and afforded the opportunity to mentor and train leaders in different countries and nations.

> 66 I PRESS TOWARD THE MARK FOR THE PRIZE
> OF THE HIGH CALLING OF GOD IN CHRIST JESUS. 99
>
> *Philippians 3:14*

CHAPTER 5
The Breakthrough
I Needed

Have you ever questioned if the Lord could use you even after all that you have been through? *"For there is no respect of persons with God."* (Romans 2:11) I heard this verse plenty of times growing up, but I didn't really think it applied to me. You see I was a saint with sinner ways. I went to church and I knew how to function in church. I could preach, pray, prophesy, and worship Jesus Christ but I had no desire to even be a preacher. My desires were full of flesh and carnality; you see if it was up to me I would have been a pornstar. I had a heavy addiction to pornography at such a young age and it was a conflict of interest with how the Lord was using me.

I remember the feeling of being ashamed, unworthy, and undeserving of God's grace, mercy, and love. I mean, could he really use someone who didn't even want to be used in the first place? "God, are you sure that you really chose me for your kingdom when I desire things that don't represent you at all?" I remember even questioning God at one point asking if he was really a God that heals and delivers then why was I so broken and damaged? You see I battled with my own issues on the inside already, but what made it worse was the people who I trusted and that were also Christians didn't make things any better. Could a preacher who not only secretly wanted to be a pornstar, but now also deal with depression really be called by God? The short answer is Yes, but the process was long and sometimes painful. Here is a small portion of my personal testimony on how the Lord showed me how he could make a sinner become a true saint.

At the tender age of eight years old I remember being exposed to pornography through an older cousin. The very first scene was life changing for me and I was hooked ever since. I remember spending most of my nights staying awake late and flicking the channel between porn and Nick at Night hoping not to get caught by my mother. The older I got the stronger the addiction grew and the more opportunities I got exposed too. Every website you can think of and DVD I could get a hold of, I had to have. Society didn't make things any better, because the more women you had the more they deemed you to be "the man". Here I was now trapped in a purpose and destiny that was never even designed for me and the worst part was it all had to be a secret because yet all the while I'm still in ministry.

My secret desire caused me to have a false pretense that the Lord was blessing me all the while it was the enemy. *"For the gifts and callings of God are without repentance."* (Romans 11:29) God makes us on purpose with a purpose you see and no matter how much I had fallen He didn't go back on his word concerning my calling. He allowed my gift to still operate and grant the people what they needed, however every platform and blessing that occurred during that time was the enemy trying to make me think I could live a double minded life forever and be blessed by God. I had to realize that although I was called by God, this gift and my character needed to be matured if I was ever going to see the real fruits in which the Lord desired for me. *"Again, the devil taketh him up into an exceeding high mountain, and sheweth him all the kingdom of the world, and the glory of them;"* (Matthew 4:8) I had to learn the hard way that the devil will also offer you blessings, platforms, opportunities, money, and the likes. I had to come to the point where I had to make a decision for myself that I was going to give in to one of the two masters. I finally came to the point in my life where I had to make a personal choice for myself and it couldn't be based on my parents, grandparents, a pastor, or anybody else but what I truly believe would be the best decision for me and according to the measure of faith that I believed.

The enemy had me as long as I kept my sin hidden. You see without accountability and honesty the enemy has free range to keep you in bondage. For years I kept my feelings bottled up. I was embarrassed, shamed, and scared. The more private I kept it, the deeper the connection grew and I found myself doing things I said I would never do. Sending nude pictures, playing sexual true or dare challenges, even found people in the church who had the same issues and we would meet to pray and watch porn. Who was this person I was becoming? Could I really fall this far away from the grace of God? Could I really let this stronghold I pray against get the best of me? Could no other prophet see what I was dealing with? I grew to understand I was allowing the power of the enemy to win because I was giving him all the tools and access he needed to stay empowered over me. *"Wherefore come out from among them, and be ye separate, saith the Lord, and touch not the unclean thing; and I will receive you."* (2 Corinthians 6:17) Your crowd matters. Your circle of influence and what you entertain all play a factor. The things that were appearing to be blessings in my life didn't matter if I had no peace of mind or comfort in my soul.

Pride will tell us that we can handle it on our own or that we don't need any help. Everything I tried of my own accord failed. Anything I put in place of my own accord I could also remove of my own accord. Cold showers, keeping busy, blocking sites; all still failed as I was just limiting the amount of usage or access I had to pornography. *"Iron sharpeneth iron; so a man sharpeneth the countenance of his friend."* (Proverbs 27:17) When I shifted my circle to those who were solid in their calling, mature in their faith, and able to be mentors and accountability partners without compromising the gospel or friendship, my stronghold started to become more and more of a thing of the past. You see it first started with making the decision that I was sick and tired of living two different lifestyles. Then I had to make the decision I couldn't do this by myself and seek the proper help I needed, be honest and open to the level of accountability, and lastly had to really understand it wasn't the end of the world but the journey I needed to take in order to mature into my calling. My fleshly desire was no longer my desire as the closer I got to the feet of Jesus understanding my relationship with him and being extended the grace and mercy. Yet, while I was a sinner there was nothing I wanted more than everything the Lord had stored up for me. During this process it was very painful. I lost a lot of friends, had family that talked about me, church folks who tried to attack me, the history of my past weighing heavy on me but the thought of my future was so much better than being stuck in this repeated cycle.

"For we walk by faith, not by sight." (2 Corinthians 5:7) I gained enough faith in the inside of me that although I was weak and powerless against this situation, the God that I serve is well, alive, real, and can do all things. I began to <u>study the word</u> like I should, <u>pray</u>, and <u>fast</u> more than I ever had at any other point in my life. I begin to take my personal relationship with Christ more seriously than before which put me in a position to allow him to have authority and control over the plans for the enemy. Things that were once hard now were becoming easier because it was the Lord doing it. Curses were being broken in my life and it didn't happen by anything that man recommended but all by the spirit of the Lord. *"For I know the thoughts that I think toward you, saith the LORD, thoughts of peace, and not of evil, to give you an expected end."* (Jeremiah 29:11 KJV) When folks would try to remind me of my mistakes, flaws, and past history I kept this verse near and dear to my heart and it just reminded me that no matter what I was going through the Lord had a plan for me and he's expecting me to make it to my destination.

Can you imagine struggling with an issue from eight years old until your mid-twenties? I mean I felt like the woman who had the issue of blood or the man who was at the pool of mercy. Stuck, lost, confused but yet somehow the Lord decides to show up strong and mighty one day and shifts my very world. To be honest I can't even tell you when the last time was the last time but all I knew it was never an issue again. All those years of secret hidden bondage while still being active in ministry. I personally would never recommend my path to anyone, the quicker you can get help do it. *"For I reckon that the suffering of this present time are not worthy to be compared with the glory which shall be revealed in us."* (Romans 8:18 KJV) The Lord supernaturally began to manifest strong in my life and ministry shortly after He delivered me. I started to make more stable connections with great influence, I gained access to different and higher-level platforms, and I saw increase and growth both in numbers and personal development.

Thirty-six states. The Lord graced me with the ability to travel and minister the word of the Lord, serve as a personal intercessor to elite celebrities in the Gospel industry. I am also a national recording artist with a prayer album, author, veteran, kingdom entrepreneur building an entire network of kingdom believers, and afforded the opportunity to mentor and train leaders in different countries and nations. If someone would have told me this was the plans God had for me when I was younger I wouldn't have believed them. Now, I know this is only the beginning of what the Lord has in store for me. *"I press toward the mark for the prize of the high calling of God in Christ Jesus."* (Philippians 3:14 KJV) I want to encourage every person to always move in a forward direction. Pursue God's purpose, and destiny because <u>what God has for you is better than anything you could envision for yourself</u>.

Moving from poverty to promise requires a lot of self action and discipline. **The biggest attack always is the one on the mind.** It's the enemy's agenda to present us with false information, wisdom and understanding.

I declare every attack of the enemy against your mind will be stopped in its tracks. I release the spirit of peace in your mind and in your home. I war in the spirit for you to break free from every warfare, struggle, and addiction. I call forth your purpose and destiny to line up and manifest. I pray in the spirit that your deliverance is for real this time with no setbacks and no failure. I decree over your life that as a son or daughter of Christ that you walk in the fullness the Lord has for you. I decree every gift will surface and be displayed to bring Glory to the kingdom of God. I declare no forces of the enemy will overthrow you and I proclaim you shall experience the goodness of the Lord all the days of your life. I pray that the blessings of the Lord release nothing but overflow into your life. May you be free by the Truth and witness a deeper connection with the Lord than ever before. May you gain wisdom, insight, direction, revelation, and knowledge to bring you into your next destination. Amos 9: 13-14 "Yes indeed, it won't be long now. God's decree.

Things are going to happen so fast your head will spin, one thing fast on the heels of the other. You won't be able to keep up. Everything will be happening at once and everywhere you look, blessings! Blessings like wine pouring off the mountains and hills. I'll make everything right again for my people Israel."

By Mike Ebron

MINISTER CENENA LOWE

Minister Cenena Lowe can be contacted on her various social media outlets.

Facebook   : Cenena HisServant Lowe 3,908 friends
Facebook page #2 : Cenena Lowe 1,242 friends
Instagram   : @ woman of youth 1,531 followers
Clubhouse   : @ Cenena Lowe 939 followers
Email   : Youthfulwoman23@gmail.com
Email address   : healingsoulsglobally@gmail.com

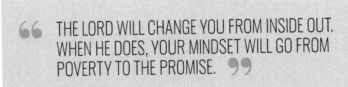

66 THE LORD WILL CHANGE YOU FROM INSIDE OUT. WHEN HE DOES, YOUR MINDSET WILL GO FROM POVERTY TO THE PROMISE. 99

CHAPTER 6

From Rejected to Redeemed

I am Minister Cenena Lowe. I was born in a little town called Amory, Mississippi on November 23, 1975. I know you are thinking, my Jesus, that was a long time ago. I was born to a teenage mother; she was only 15 when she birthed me out of her womb. I always say I was rejected from my mother's womb, but I now know that the rejection was a redirect for my life. I say that because my guardianship shifted, and I ended up being raised by my grandmother. I believe that it was God's way of protecting me and that it made me who I am today.

I am a mother of twin boys and a daughter. I am appointed for such a time as this. I am the Visionary of Women of Youth Outreach Ministries founded in 2014. I have been called by God to teach and preach a life changing word of Jesus Christ to the World. I am a mother who has a loving, caring demeanor, and a passion for people of all walks of life with an intense love for family. I have a special anointing for women. Since 2014, I have been focusing on leading women out of spiritual bondage and into wholeness while striving to be a virtuous woman and yielding to God. I am on an assignment to build God's people through preaching, teaching and prophesying as well as sharing his love to his people. I am to be a light to a dark and hurting world.

I have experienced feeling empty for as long as I remember. Several things happen when you experience emptiness. You find yourself in relationships you should never be in. You tend to please others when you are not pleased. You give your most intimate part of yourself to other people who do not deserve it. I had to come to myself and learn to love myself realizing that after being rejected, it takes time to learn and know your worth. When you don't know who you truly are, you look for love in all the wrong places, people, and things. Looking back, my struggles showed that the Lord always had his hand on me. He had a promise for my life. You may have struggles right now, but God has a plan for your life. He has a promise of redemption for your life in Him. You must know that there is a plan and a promise for your life even in the times of hurt, pain, disappointments, and struggles. Know that you can do all things through Christ who strengthens you. We all have struggles. I have had many. I can reflect on a conversation with some friends that pulled me into a life of perversion which came after coming out of an abusive marriage. You may be wondering what I mean by a lifestyle of perversion. What I mean is just through a conversation, something I never thought about was planted into my thoughts. I began to live a lifestyle as a lesbian for many years. Over ten years to be exact. Deception has a way of creeping through a door even though you are in church singing in the choir and going to a holiness church with your skirt long enough to touch the floor. The enemy does not care anything about your denomination or title. I was introduced to the lifestyle through a conversation between myself and three other friends that had encountered this lifestyle. I know you might think this is crazy. Although the ladies were younger than I was, they shared their experiences that pulled me in. Even in my hesitation, they said DO NOT KNOCK IT UNTIL YOU TRY IT. That was it. I gave in to the devil although I knew it was wrong. I didn't hate homosexuals, but I knew it was wrong. I definitely didn't agree with the lifestyle. Remember, if you ever give room to the devil, he will take over the whole house for sure.

I had no idea that I would look at women differently after this encounter with my attraction to the same sex. When you are in sin, it feels so right, although God clearly lets us know that it is an abomination in his eyesight. I know people will think I am crazy when I say God allowed me to go through lesbianism so I could come out to tell the story and show someone that He will deliver and will always give you a way of escape. Needless to say, he gave me that just in the nick of time. Although I left church for years, I eventually went back and the Lord began to do a work in me. Yes, in me. He promised, He would never leave or forsake me and He definitely covered me in my darkest hour. God is so AMAZING. He will use the very thing you struggled with and had you bound, to help set others free. He is a promise keeping God. He said he would perfect everything concerning you. It concerns Him if it concerns you because He loves you just that much. You don't have to be perfect for Jesus to love you or for him to be concerned about you. I just want to encourage you as you read my testimony. Jesus loves you just the way you are. The Lord snatched me out of the hands of the enemy because His hands aren't too short that He can't save you. His promises are **YES** and **AMEN**. I had to step out and trust him. I had to learn to love myself after realizing how much Jesus loved me. Thank God for Jesus. He knows our hearts.

I started with my testimony to show that there is no sin too great for God to deliver you from and to turn your life around. It starts with changing your mindset and believing that you are worthy of God's grace and mercy. My mindset changed along the way after coming to Christ. I am in a better place now and as I write, I reflect on where my life was after birthing my twins. I was in low-income housing, living in poverty. I didn't have help from my children's father, and I didn't trust anyone babysitting my twins. I ended up on food stamps and received a monthly check through the welfare department (Department of Human Services) here in Mississippi. I utilized this assistance until 2015 which was the year I cut off the use of food stamps. In 2017 I cut off the use of Section 8 housing assistance. It has been a struggle, I must say. I remember asking God, "How can I say I trust you and be on the government system when I was born to be on the Kingdom's system. I didn't think that I deserved anything better until I later realized I didn't want to be on governmental assistance for the rest of my life. I cut everything off and never looked back. I have since moved forward to the promised land.

Living a lifestyle of poverty, I know it is a mindset. You have to choose to change your way of thinking. Everything starts in the mind, and you can choose to manage things in your life better. I told you previously that I was raised by my grandmother who passed away December 2020. We lived in what others might call the "Projects". I never realized we were poor. I actually thought we were rich because I wanted for nothing and the area that we lived in was not bad at all. We didn't have a lot of crime in our town, so thank God for that. I know one thing: we were so blessed because as time went on and I grew up, I discovered most of my clothes were coming from yard sales. They only looked very expensive because my grandmother worked at a dry cleaner and would keep them washed and pressed. This would give them a good ole crisp and brand-new look. She was a woman who knew how to turn little into much, and a praying woman she was. Of course, we had to go to church on Sundays and she was faithful with her little in paying her tithes and offering. I do know this is why we never went without. I learned as I grew to be a young adult, that she was great at budgeting which took me years to get to because of habits that I picked up along the way. When I came over to the Lord's side, I realized that the Lord wants us to be faithful over the little so that he can make us ruler of much, and to be a great steward over what he gives us. I have learned to make sacrifices over the years and because of that, I have nothing lacking, missing, or broken due to the mishandling of what he blesses me with. This was definitely a process and took time because I was a habitual gambler, but the Lord will change you from inside out. When He does, your mindset will go from Poverty to the Promise.

SYDNEY ADU-AKORSAH

My name is Sydney Adu-Akorsah and I am a young man after the heart of God who currently resides in Hyattsville, Maryland. I am also a recent first-generation college graduate and I have my Bachelor's Degree in Business Administration. My walk with God has not been easy and I do not have it all together, but I have a God whose strength is made perfect in our weaknesses. My faith took a leap last year during COVID, and ever since I have been striving to be on fire for the Lord and not being lukewarm. I am originally from Ghana, but I grew up in the northside of Chicago for the majority of my life. God has delivered me from many addictions, and he is still delivering me from my past. I also serve under the leadership of my mentor Apostle Mike Ebron Jr's Prayer Club Ministry, and I am extremely humbled and grateful to have an opportunity to tell my story.

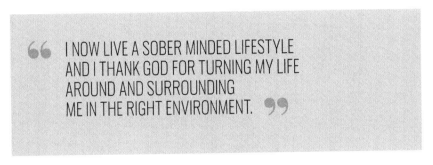

66 I NOW LIVE A SOBER MINDED LIFESTYLE AND I THANK GOD FOR TURNING MY LIFE AROUND AND SURROUNDING ME IN THE RIGHT ENVIRONMENT. 99

CHAPTER 7
Miracle in the Night

My name is Sydney Adu-Akorsah and I am originally from Accra, Ghana. I have two siblings, an older, and younger brother making me the middle child. My parents moved to the United States shortly after my birth and we lived in Minnesota until I was four years old. My parents got divorced when I was four which caused me and my brothers to move back to Ghana with my mom. I come from a single parent background with no support from my biological father. I lived in Ghana for six years and returned to the United States to live in Chicago, Illinois with my former step dad when I was ten years old. I lived in the northside of Chicago for eight and a half years and it is the longest I have ever lived in one location. I moved out of Chicago in 2016, and I have bounced around living in four different states over the past four years.

During the time span of me moving across different states, I graduated from Holy Trinity High School in 2016, and decided to attend Indiana State University. I graduated from Indiana State University on May 8th, 2021, and I am a first-generation college graduate in my family. I had 3 major changes in college and decided to finally pursue my bachelor's degree in Business Administration. My faith in God started to grow while I was away in college. I was extremely blessed to have people that had a genuine love of God that sparked some fire in me to fully commit to the Lord while in college. I was heavily involved in the church at a young age and went to church faithfully in middle school. Once I gained more freedom in high school, church was not really a priority for me and I attended occasionally, however I always made time to pray and my belief in God never faded away.

My love for the Lord first developed when I was a young child. I was pushed by my mom, and my late grandmother as a kid to make God my number one priority. My late grandmother was my biggest "hype man" when I was younger. She would always refer to me as either Pastor, or Doctor Sydney. I would like to humbly state that I was her favorite grandchild and always found such great favor from her which I never understood as a child. Looking back now as a young adult I can now see that at a young age my grandmother saw something great in me that till this day I am still trying to figure out what was so special about me as a kid. My connection with God was at an all-time high as a young child. It was normal for me to have different types of supernatural encounters with God as well as dreams.

My childhood years were mostly spent in Ghana from age four to ten. During the six-year span I spent in Ghana, life was challenging and tough especially for my mom. My mom had to take care of three boys while working as an entrepreneur and owning her own business as a single parent. Although we found life challenging, my mom always found favor from God in the struggle. I am very blessed to have a God-fearing mom that wants the best for all her children. I have personally witnessed my mom sacrifice, living a luxurious lifestyle and sacrificing her own personal desires just to see all of us prosper as her children. I remember there were times when I needed money to go to school in Ghana and my mom would scrape up all her change she had just so that I could have enough to buy some food.

Despite our early struggles in Ghana our life started changing for the better after a few years of fully settling. God blessed my mom with a great mind to operate in different business sectors. Over the years my mom was able to develop real estate on the side. I watched her build a mansion for the family from the ground up and it was truly remarkable. We eventually settled into the new family mansion which was a huge upgrade from where we were originally staying in Ghana. The new family house was also in a top-class neighborhood in Ghana, and I thank God for the huge turnaround we had while living in Ghana. My family started out with humble beginnings in our first few years in Ghana, and then God supernaturally turned it around and positioned us to live in the biggest house we had ever lived in as a family in a top-class neighborhood.

The family was finally starting to pick up some momentum, although we still had some struggles. My family does not come from money but what I can say is that we have found great favor from God. As things were going in the right direction for the family my mom decided to settle with my former step dad whom she met in Ghana. He resided in Chicago. I remember coming home from school one day around November of 2008 and my mom told me that I would be returning back to the United States to live with my former stepdad in Chicago. My older brother had already left to stay in Chicago about a month before I did. After hearing the news I was super ecstatic to have the opportunity to live in the States and sad because I was leaving my childhood friends behind.

In December of 2008 at 10 years old I journeyed from Ghana and flew by myself to the United States. I arrived at the perfect time in the cold winter of the Windy City. During my time in Ghana, I always envisioned the United States as everyone living the American Dream with little to no struggle as I was used to watching in the movies, however I was in for a rude awakening. I went from living in a mansion, having a maid, and doing little to no work in Ghana to living in a small one-bedroom apartment in Chicago sharing a small bed with my older brother and my former stepdad. I laugh about it today as I reminisce, but I sure was not laughing then. Life was very challenging for me when I first arrived in the United States. I was so used to the privileged lifestyle I had in Ghana, and I barely broke a sweat, but when I came to the United States, I had to actually do things for myself for the first time in my life. My time in the United States has humbled me in a good way and I am very grateful for it.

As I began to adjust and become accustomed to the American lifestyle my connection with God began to dwindle and going to church did not become an obligation for me in high school, however during middle school I went to church consistently. My former step dad hardly ever attended church and since my mom stayed in Ghana, going to church was never really enforced in the household. The further I got away from God the more I began to gravitate towards sin. In high school I struggled with extreme low self-esteem, low confidence, depression, anxiety, bitterness, abandonment issues, pornography, and masturbation. To cope with my internal issues, prayer, and basketball became my escape. I was very fortunate to play basketball for all four years in high school. It was a very dark time for me, however I thank God for never taking his hands off me.

In college I became more lost than ever in finding my identity and I completely lost my way. I was no longer a basketball athlete like I was in high school, and I was on my own. I barely read the Bible, and the only time I ever turned to it was when I was in great desperation. Fortunately for me I was blessed to have an upperclassman connect me back to God, and for the first time in years I began to develop a hunger for the Lord, however, I developed bad drinking habits, as well as partying. I went out to parties almost every weekend, and I drank alcohol very heavily. My life was slowly spiraling for the worst, then one day in December of 2019, after coming home from the bar, I fell asleep, and I heard the voice of the Lord clearly and audibly in my dream. It is till this day one of the craziest supernatural encounters I have ever had. God's voice is so calm and peaceful but powerful at the same time. That day in 2019 changed my life forever and I began to slowly cut back on some bad habits.

In 2020 during COVID, I began having the craziest supernatural dreams and encounters with God. Through these encounters with God in my dreams my faith has been transformed to another level, and it has fueled me to pursue God even more. The pandemic also showed me to have patience with God and trust in his timing because what the Lord gives, He can also take away. I am learning to not take life for granted. The Lord also delivered me from pornography, masturbation, and heavy alcohol drinking, which were the three main areas that was dictating my life. I thank God for delivering me from my bad habits as I am still healing every day from my past mistakes. I am very glad that the Lord listened to my prayers and delivered me from the major addictions that were controlling my life. I now live a sober minded lifestyle and I thank God for turning my life around and surrounding me in the right environment.

By Sydney Adu-Akorsah

EVANGELIST DOROTHY FISHER

Evangelist Dorothy Fisher encourages you to take advantage of reading her upcoming books entitled,

- JEALOUSY, A spirit of deceit A must read book
- From Pride to Humility ANGER, Another spirit of deceit A must read book

Purchase books at www.dorothyhelingschool.com or Amazon stores:

Contact and support Evangelist Fisher by visiting:
www.dorothyhealingscool.com
&
Dorothy's Healing School Of Ministry Facebook Page
YouTube Channel
This book is copyright protected.

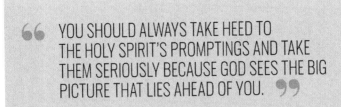

66 YOU SHOULD ALWAYS TAKE HEED TO THE HOLY SPIRIT'S PROMPTINGS AND TAKE THEM SERIOUSLY BECAUSE GOD SEES THE BIG PICTURE THAT LIES AHEAD OF YOU. 99

CHAPTER 8

The Enemy Asked for My Mind, but God Said "No"

In January of 2019, I began my journey to having a renewed mind in Christ. I attended church faithfully for many years, but I was hell bound because I did not have a renewed mind. For 10-12 years, the Lord tugged at my heart for me to have the mind of Christ as it is written in Philippians 2: 5-8 KJV, *"Let this mind be in you, which was also in Christ Jesus"*. I didn't know what all of that meant and didn't respond properly to the Holy Spirit promptings.

In the year of 2018, I began to hear clearly within my inner man that a spirit of jealousy was trying to attach itself to my life. I examined my heart, and I was unable to find who or what I was jealous of. As time went by I began to hear stronger and stronger in my heart the Holy Spirit prompting regarding the spirit of jealousy trying to attach itself to my life. I couldn't help wondering if it was really me jealous or was it someone who had a jealous spirit toward me.

I did not realize how serious the spirit of jealousy was until one day, that evil spirit rose up in me, pronouncing evil thoughts in my mind for me to repeat and act upon. Immediately, I knew that was not the right thing for me to say, do, or feel as the spirit was not from God. Immediately, I cast down that evil spirit and thought from my mind, if I had ignorantly acted upon those evil thoughts and words, that deceitful spirit of jealousy would have entered into my heart to take control and ruin my life, destiny and future. It would have attempted to ruin my relationship with those who were important to me, my husband, my family and friends, or anyone who may have stood in a way of opposition to me.

Not knowing exactly where this evil spirit came from or why it had attached itself to my life, I began seriously to search my heart, meditate on God's Word, and ask the Holy Spirit to show me my error(s). I did not want the spirit of jealousy to enter into my heart and to take control of my life. It is not good to be ignorant to the spirit of jealousy, the spirit of deceit, of how it operates, because the enemy uses your ignorance against you to destroy you for his evil pleasure and purpose.

As time went by I began to pay closer attention to my personal life and draw closer to God and His Word. The Holy Spirit began to remove the scales from my eyes and reveal to me the hidden evilness of the spirit of jealousy that the enemy planned to use against me. I actually saw in the spirit realm demonic activities in action to carry out their evil plan against me, and boy this did not make the devil happy, as my heart had become enlightened to the craftiness and truth of his evil plans. The enemy got madder and became more aggressive in his attacks against me, to defeat me and to take over my mind..."But greater is he that is in you, than he that is in the world" (1 John 4:4 KJV). God was on my side.

It is amazing how the enemy tries to do his evil work when you take little notice or attention to his actions or when you are vulnerable, such as when you are sick or you are asleep in bed. That is how the enemy works, sneaky and cunningly. The enemy knows that if he comes straight at you and not cunningly, he would be caught red-handed and defeated on the spot. As stated earlier, the enemy was not through with me, but he became stronger and more aggressive in his attacks against me, especially during my sleep time.

One special night in 2019, as I lay partially asleep in bed, I had a tugging at my body, tapping on my legs and feet, to get up and pray. (I realized later they were the angels of the Lord). However, I ignored the tugging and tapping to my body because I wanted to sleep. I wasn't aware that the enemy had devised a plan to take away my mind that night, but the Holy Spirit did. That is why I was beckoned to get up and pray, but I nicely refused and turned over in bed to finish sleeping.

On that night in 2019, as I continued to lie partially asleep in bed, all of a sudden, just as it was with Adam and Eve in the Garden of Eden (in Genesis 3:7) when their eyes became open (to evil), a quick change took place in my heart, and my eyes became open in the spirit realm. I saw darkness, demonic activities taking place in my mind and as the demonic spirits saw that I took notice of them, they stood up and fought speedily against my mind to quickly gain control of it.

I was totally lost to myself as to what to do next. I looked inside the walls of my heart for answers, only to find out that it was empty and dark. I became very nervous and frightened at what was happening to me. I tried to understand but there was nothing for me to understand, to reason or to know, because it was as if I already knew everything in eternity that I needed to know and understand and that too ran out. That may sound odd, but it was true, there was nothing left in eternity for me to know, or at least that is how I felt in my state of mind from the spirit of pride.

Everything was happening so fast I didn't know how to prevent what was happening to me. I was scared and cried out softly to God for help, and behold, I happened to look down by the side of my bed and saw two angels that were pulling on my arms and beckoning me to get up and follow them. The angels of the Lord, help pulled me up,

rushed me to the living room, and quickly pushed me to the floor on my bent knees and directed me to bow my head and hands to the ground and I began to worship the Lord. It was in this state of posture that I began to find comfort, peace and security in the Lord of not being mentally lost, against the assigned attack of the enemy against my mind.

What a night and experience to remember! I stayed in my posture of worship until the break of day, and then began to read my Bible and meditate on God's Word all into the next day and days afterwards. The Holy Spirit began to teach me how to humble myself, and began to show me that it was the spirit of pride that opened the door for the spirit of jealousy to attach itself to my life. The spirit of pride is also a spirit of deceit. It was a few months later before I had some understanding of what took place in my mind and body on that night. With the spirit of pride, the enemy was trying to make me snap, to have a mental breakdown; to take over my life, but God said "no". I was very shocked at what took place in my life on that night, as I considered myself a person of prayer and always in guard of my heart. But not so, the enemy had devised a plan against me to take away my mind that night, as I had got to a point where I was very hungry for God and His Word and only wanted to do His Will. The enemy's sole purpose was to stop me from fulfilling God's destiny for my life.

From my experience, I learned that it is not only good for you to examine your own heart, but it is also wise to ask God to search your heart daily to see if there is anything wicked in it. The enemy is out to take your mind that he may control it. If he takes your mind, the enemy knows that you are a defeated foe. And then he and his army of demons sit back and laugh and say "she is crazy, hadn't you heard that she has lost her mind and she is supposed to be holy, ha.ha.ha". I can only imagine what mental or nervous breakdowns people go through. It is a very serious and scary experience for them. They feel lost in a world of their own with no room for hope. Only God can deliver you from the attack of the enemy on your mind for whatever the reason may be. The enemy asked to take over my mind, but God said "No". It was there where I began my journey from an unrenewed mind to a renewed mind in Christ. What a day of victory!

In conclusion, when you have come to the end of the prideful spirit that is in your life, there is nothing else for you to hold onto. There is no more understanding to grab and hold onto, no more wisdom to ravish and hold onto, no more glory for you to obtain and hold onto. When the spirit of pride (a false god) enters into your heart and controls your life, you are left to fall. You lose mental control of your life. Your faculties are suspended. It is what people call "crazy or having a nervous breakdown". You are bowed in a fetal position, crying, trembling, shaking, looking lost and confused because you are at your wits end. You are in a very dark place in your life because you no longer have control of your understanding of what to do next or where to turn. The false god of pride has robbed you of your understanding.

Realize as a human being, there is an end to you knowing everything because you are not the All-Knowing God. The enemy succumbs you in pride to know everything "I know, I know", but at the other end of pride is a dark place "where everything you knew you don't know anymore. Your knowledge has come to a dead end. Your understanding is suspended". This is the cunning part of the enemy. He, cunningly and subtly, will have you yield to prideful things, slowly and gradually setting you up for the big fall in your life, as he did with Adam and Eve in the garden of Eden. Unfortunately, the enemy doesn't tell you that you will eventually come to the end of the road of pride and fall off the cliff. That is exactly what the spirit of pride did to King Nebuchadnezzar in the book of the bible, Daniel 4:24-37. King Nebuchadnezzar thought he was like God in that he had all power and wisdom to get anything he wanted, because he had accumulated great wealth, power and fame. As King Nebuchadnezzar failed to call on and acknowledge God as the Only One who gives wisdom, power, and wealth, one day, all of a sudden, the enemy came and took over his mind, and he began to act and live in the wilderness as a wild animal for seven years.

Like King Nebuchadnezzar, others have lost their mind (understanding) to the hideous danger of the spirit of pride. They did not realize that on the other end of the spectrum of pride is «a lost mind that doesn't know what to do". You are mentally insane. I believe had King Nebuchadnezzar known about the deceitful and dangerous spirit of pride, he would have humbled himself and called on the Almighty God. The spirit of pride is a spirit of deceit, and unknowingly to God's people, many walk in it blindly. The spirit of pride, if not dealt with properly, leads you to a fall, often losing your mind or having a nervous breakdown. I thank God for His mercy and grace, that He allowed neither to happen to me, but God left me to tell my story to help those who may be on the wrong path to pride.

Last, in my thirst for understanding, I asked God the question, "why do people lose their minds?" I began to understand from God, that the Holy Spirit always gives warnings, but people hardened their hearts to the continuous promptings of the Holy Spirit in their spirit. Sometimes it may be done out of ignorance, and people ignore or take lightly to the promptings by the Holy Spirit and deny the seriousness thereof to the issues at hand. People may ignore the Holy Spirit promptings, such as to renew the mind, don't see yourself as better than others and judge others (which is a deadly sin as the sin of adultery), put away jealousy and strife, love one another as Christ loves you. These can be advance notices or warnings given to you by the Holy Spirit, but if you ignore the warnings, the issues are bound to become something big and out of control. You should always take heed to the Holy Spirit promptings and take them seriously because God sees the big picture that lies ahead of you.

Today, the word of God says in Hebrews 3:15, *"Today, if you hear his voice, don't harden your hearts as Israel did when they rebelled"* (NLT). In other words, don't rebel but take heed to the Word of God. Whenever the Holy Spirit tugs at your heart, no matter how small or minor the issue may seem to you, stop immediately and address the issue right then. Take heed to the Holy Spirit prompting, whether it be for you to have a renewed mind, be generous, be kind, or whatever. It is for your own good. I pray by the Word of God that the sharing of my story has touched your heart in some way for the better. If so, please share your testimony at sharemytestimonynow@gmail.com.

JACYNTHIA BAILEY

JaCynthia Bailey is a North Carolina native, she has been serving in ministry for over 8 years in many different capacities, she is a wife to an amazing Pastor in the Methodist Church and a mother of 3 amazing children. She is the founder of InTouch Day Retreats which have turned into weekend and couple retreats. JaCynthia has a passion for the supernatural and for helping God's children get back to who He's created them to be. JaCynthia loves encouraging youth and Women in the things of the Lord. She works full time in the tech Industry, and shares the Gospel in schools, retreats, online events and anywhere God leads!

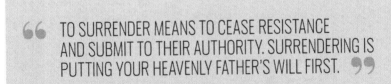

TO SURRENDER MEANS TO CEASE RESISTANCE AND SUBMIT TO THEIR AUTHORITY. SURRENDERING IS PUTTING YOUR HEAVENLY FATHER'S WILL FIRST.

CHAPTER 9

Everything You Ever Wanted

Have you ever been in a situation where you weren't quite sure how it was going to turn out? Let's just keep it real (if we're honest, that was all of us in the crazy upside down year of 2020) Speaking of 2020, I want to share what was taking place in my life that particular summer. A few days before August 2020, through a series of unfortunate events my husband & I found ourselves faced with the fact that his paycheck for August was going to be nine hundred and fifty dollars.

To put it in perspective, our monthly household budget at this time was thirty-five hundred dollars.

We learned to live off of his income. My random paychecks from real estate sales and side jobs went towards debt & family fun, but the week we got the news of his lower pay all of my possible real estate deals I had were falling apart. The only sure thing in front of us was $950. Needless to say, tensions in our household began making its way to the surface; my husband wanted me to make our usual budget & I really didn't feel the need.

On August 1st I woke up early & prayed. I thanked God for everything He was doing & how He's always provided for my family. It became clear to me in my prayer time that if I really trusted God and if I really wanted to show Him how thankful I was, I should walk into the month of August faithfully. I told my husband, "Babe, this month I'm keeping a record of all the blessings we receive!" I'm sure he didn't really know what to do with this declaration I had made, so he smiled and said, "Ok".

As I opened the notes tab on my phone and began to type, the first blessing that came to mind was the grades that had rolled out that morning from my three summer classes: all A's. (Friends I have three kids who were all at home during the pandemic, and I made all A's blessings right!?) I felt God speak to my heart, "JaCynthia I AM The Shepherd. I will provide and I will bless your hands."

Boldly, I faithfully paid our tithes for the usual amount, I gave it to a friend's school in need, in Zimbabwe and then I went to work. Each morning I started off being thankful, I looked for & expected Him, I asked God to bless the work from my side gig of delivering groceries. Each day was filled with blessings from a friend sending $100 dollars, to God's protection from a hydroplaning car coming towards me, to $40 tips on multiple occasions. We had the gift of unplanned family time in the mountains. A random investment account sent me a statement which had grown over $1,200 from a one-time investment. Moreover, a friend compensated me for handling the documentation of selling their home.

I could keep going...but what I took to heart for August 2020; God wants to show up for his children. He is the Master of

Peace if we keep our focus on Him. My Heavenly Father reminded me that He comes in unexpected ways and my job is to work with what He's placed before me and simply trust him. Act in faith. I don't need to know the plan because **He's the Shepherd and I'm the sheep**. I just need to keep getting to know His voice & follow it. I just need to surrender.

On September 1st, I printed and read each blessing out loud to my husband. He sat in awe and gave looks of shock, as if he hadn't been there for each step. It reminded me that we can get so busy, we don't even realize just how much God brings us through.

Our list for August is filled with things that didn't have a numerical value, those blessings filled me with joy, peace & raised my faith. But you've read to this point and God deserves all the glory, so I'll share the grand total of our August 2020 financial blessings: $5,913.10.

Fast forward a bit, I kept surrendering and seeking God's will for my life, and for my family. He led me to double up on classes and finish a semester early, (people thought I was crazy, you're in a pandemic, take your time with school, but I followed my Father's instructions.) I graduated in December of 2020. He told me to leave real estate, my main source of income & start retreats for women teaching them the lessons I walked through with Him. I went from cutting off my income to spending upfront money for monthly retreats. As I stepped out, and kept my heart in a posture of thanksgiving, He literally downloaded every plan, every detail, sent the help, and provided every dollar that was needed.

He brought divine connections into my life and with every experience I grew in my knowledge and understanding of who He is as a Shepherd. Each month required more surrendering, to be able to hear his voice clearly. Ever since August, I have reached new levels of faith and I am more convinced than ever that He will show you how.

In February of 2021, He gave me the exact job with the exact pay that I asked for! (Sidebar: that job journey is a whole other testimony that deserves its own book!)

He is a good, good father, and after this past year of walking with Him, watching Him answer prayers, and reveal His plans for my life, I'm a living witness that everything you've ever wanted, desired or dreamed about is on the other side of your thanksgiving, your obedience and your surrender.

Let's break those three action steps down.

THANKSGIVING:

For me I had to quickly focus on what God was already doing in my life, that August of writing down each blessing no matter how small or big cultivated such a rich awareness. Being mindful of my blessings kept me expecting, it kept me humble, and it kept my eyes on my Shepherd.

OBEDIENCE:

So often in church settings we hear obedience is better than sacrifice. I want to submit to you friends to examine those small simple areas in your life. Are you being obedient to the word of God? Loving your neighbor as yourself, reading His word, praying continuously, counting it all joy.... Take time to examine yourself & choose to offer your obedience in a new way. Walk with Him and partner with Him so that you may have His guidance and the peace that comes with it!

SURRENDERING:

I'm going to keep it real honest friends, surrendering took me years. It's the denying of self, and honoring God's will above my own part that kept tripping me up. I heard this statement once: "We want to control what we do not respect." That statement shook me, I mean, My God, I don't want to control my own life, I respect Him as my Shepherd, as my Creator, as My Father who knows all.

Jesus was our perfect example in this matter. Jesus was fully surrendered, and He performed miracles. <u>To surrender means to cease resistance and submit to their authority. Surrendering is putting your Heavenly Father's will first.</u>

LASTLY

For anyone who's curious the blessings have doubled and I'm still in awe of this great amazing God we serve!

SCRIPTURES TO PRAY WITH:

1 Thessalonians 5:16-18 KJV
>   -*Continually give thanks in all circumstances*

Colossians 2:6-7 KJV
>   -*So, walk in Him, rooted and built up in Him and established in the faith, as you have been taught, abounding in it with thanksgiving*

Deuteronomy 28:12 KJV
>   -*Bless the work of your hands*

John 14:27 KJV
>   -*My peace I leave you*

Exodus 19:5 KJV
>   -*Now therefore, if ye will obey my voice indeed, and keep my covenant, then ye shall be a peculiar treasure unto me above all people: for all the earth is mine*

Proverbs 23:26 KJV
>   -*My son, give me your heart, and let your eyes observe my ways.*

1 Samuel 15:22 NLT
>   -*But Samuel replied, "What is more pleasing to the LORD: your burnt offerings and sacrifices or your obedience to his voice? Listen! Obedience is better than sacrifice, and submission is better than offering the fat of rams.*

Sending Love & God's encouragement your way

NATALIE BATISTE

I am Natalie Batiste, and I am from Opelousas, Louisiana. I have been living in Opelousas for 29 years. I am the mother of one beautiful princess Sarai Batiste. I have my Associate's Degree in General Studies and bachelor's degree in child and family studies minor psychology. I am currently a Preschool Teacher in Lafayette, LA. I am a Paparazzi Independent Business Consultant and have been in the business for over a year now. I am also a prophetic worship dancer. Worship is my name, it's my place where I break-free.

Facebook Business: Queen Bling of Hope
Website: https://paparazziaccessories.com/342349
Facebook: Daughter of Worship

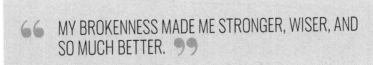

66 MY BROKENNESS MADE ME STRONGER, WISER, AND SO MUCH BETTER. 99

CHAPTER 10

My Testimony

So glad I made it. I never thought I would be here today writing some of my testimony. I was a child that went through many struggles but one thing I kept with me as I went through was God. My journey wasn't easy. One day I was like, God, I cannot keep doing things that are not pleasing to you...trail riding, toxic friendships, brokenness, depressions, discouraged, and relationships that weren't for me. I still gave in to my God and knew that wasn't the way for me but that was the route I had to go through to testify and tell my story. One thing I did and didn't stop was I still pressed my way to the house of the Lord.

No matter how hard you try to run away from God He knows how to get your attention. I experienced a time when I was in my teenage years where I surrendered and gave my life to the Lord for real at the age of 14. I remember at the age 0f 14 I started to dance and took the responsibility to carry the assignment. Ever since I accepted the assignment over my life, I have not been the same. By surrendering my life to God completely I was able to see God's hands upon my life like never before, as I began to worship, seek, pray, fast and let God be God in my life. When God is in need of you (no matter your faults), He still wants to use you for his glory so you can be a living testimony to what Heaven has announced. My God! As I continued to worship and consecrate before the Lord, my life would never be the same as I do what God has for me to do. Never think you are too late to surrender your life to God. Just know that God wants to love you. Make the choice today and say, *"God I totally surrender and today I give my life totally to you. Take full control of my life today, Not my will but your will be done in Jesus name. Amen."*

DEPRESSION

I could remember one occasion being depressed to the point I wanted to have a mental breakdown, crying out on the side of my bed and saying, I wanted God to take all the pain away to the point that I felt I didn't want to be here anymore, and say forget about everything. Oh but that same day my beautiful princess Sarai said, "Mommie I want to listen to the song `Something Has to Break by Kierra Sheard" and immediately as the song begin to play the weight of everything I was feeling all over me immediately "BROKE," aye Jesus. I could not stop thanking God for that moment. I know that no matter what, when God gives you a sign, be obedient and don't question it because God definitely will see you through it all. On another occasion I was literally on my living room floor weeping uncontrollably and I could not do anything else but pour out my tears and had my hands on my head and immediately God gave me relief and said daughter I got you. Psalm 34:17-18 says, *"The righteous cry out, and the Lord hears them; he delivers them from all their troubles. The Lord is close to the brokenhearted and saves those who are crushed in spirit."*

I thank God for the word declared in Deuteronomy 31:6 that says, *"Be strong and courageous. Do not be afraid or terrified because of them, for the LORD your God goes with you; He will never leave you nor forsake you.»* My God! In the word de*press* it shows Press, so no matter what comes my way I had to **PRESS**.

DISCOURAGED

I can recall a time in my life as a little girl going through school that I pushed through no matter what the people had claimed in my life. I knew how hard my classes were and had to work extra hard to get the grades I knew that I was capable of getting. Being diagnosed with dyslexia, I didn't let that keep me down or break me. Throughout my life, dyslexia couldn't hold me back. I wouldn't allow it. *No one will be able to stand against you all the days of your life. As I was with Moses, so I will be with you; I will never leave you nor forsake you. (Joshua 1:9)*

I pressed and worked hard and got my schoolwork done. Like I stated before, sometimes I had to work harder in one class than the others because some material was more intense to understand than others, but I pressed through it. Discouragement couldn't keep me down in the name of Jesus. I also experienced different series while in college. I could recall a time when I had to study for a final and Lord knows I studied until I couldn't study any more. I'm here to let someone know that "FAILURE IS NOT AN OPTION." Why? I'm glad you ask because every exam I took for that class I failed it. I was like," but God, I'm trying my hardest to understand the material but I'm having a hard time understanding it." Let me say this there's always a ram in the bush, to let you know that God is with you wherever you go. I can recall sitting in my professor's office as we began to go over the questions and answers. Now mind you I went back home and studied and studied and studied and told myself I couldn't study any more. When I went in to take the final, I said God you handle this one and bring back everything I need to remember. Philippians 4:13 KJV says, *"I can do all things through Christ that strengthens me"* and this was the only class that I was waiting for to get the final grade. When I received the grade I began to praise God like never before because it was the only class that I was worried about and God word declares in Proverbs 3:5-6 KJV, *"Trust in the Lord with all your heart and lean not to your own understanding but in all your ways acknowledge him and he will direct your paths."*

Another moment in college was when I was going through a horrible moment in my life with family to the point I didn't know if I was going to be okay from discouragement hitting me so hard that every day tears were rolling uncontrollably. I was waking up with bags under my eyes. My GPA was a 0.003 in that semester and all I could do was cry, but I was reminded that again Philippians 4:13 KJV declares, *"I can do all things through Christ that strengthens me"*: that stayed with me through it all. The next semester I came back STRONG and finished with a 3.2. Thank you Jesus, you did it again for me. I come to let anyone that is facing dyslexia know that is not your stopping point because there is more that God has for you and you will get through it by standing on the word of God and praying. Can you handle the pressure? Yes you can, because God was with me and he gives the strongest battles to his warriors that can handle the pressure? So, no matter how down you feel you always can look to Jesus and He will bring you through it all. In Isaiah 41:10 KJV the word says, *"fear not, for I am with you; be not dismayed, for I am your God; I will strengthen you, I will help you, I will uphold you with my righteous right hand."*

BROKENNESS

This one hit is different because a song flashes before me and the song is "Broken" by Shekinah Glory Ministry. I was broken into pieces that shattered me to the cord that I couldn't even come to grip. Tears were unstoppable from the hurt that broke me down. All I could say was Jesus rescued me like never before. I felt his touch like never before, Ahhhh...Jesus! Psalm 107:28 KJV says, *"Then they cried to the Lord in their trouble, and he delivered them from their distress."* As I was continuing to go through my brokenness this song "BROKEN" touched my soul on different levels and God spoke loud and clear to me through this song.

I been broken and bruised
Wondering will God still use
Crying out to you
Got nothing left to lose
Father hear my plea
Need You to rescue me
'Cause I'm broken"
(Shekinah Glory Ministry, 2012)

I keep repeating these lines over and over and then this another part of the song that touched me,

> *I've got something to say*
> *Not sure where I start*
> *I'm afraid to begin it's all falling apart*
> *See I thought because I was working For You*
> *Everything wrong You would undo*
> *But it wasn't quite true*
> *It's hard to admit*
> *That I can't feel you like I use too*
> *'Cause I'm in ministry and I'm messed up*
> *I'm confused with no one to turn to*
> *I need a breakthrough, I need a breakthrough*
> *'Cause this the thing You've anointed me to do*
> **(Shekinah Glory Ministry, 2012)**

Overall, through my journey as I have shared some of my testimony, my prayer is that someone will be changed and be made whole. No matter what comes in life, know that God will surpass the depression and peace will be your portion in the name of Jesus. Know that depression can't keep you down and it has to bow in the name of Jesus. In John 16:33 (KJV), the word says *"I have said these things to you, that in me you may have peace. In the world you will have tribulation. But take heart; I have overcome the world."* Discouragement came but it couldn't keep me down in the name of Jesus. As I look back, I had to go through the discouragement not to break me but to equip me for what is ahead of me. Jeremiah 29:11 (NIV) says, *"For I know the plans I have for you,"* declares the LORD, plans to prosper you *and not to harm you, plans to give you hope and a future."* In the midst of every tear I cried it was just squeezing out every failure and I knew I was going to come out with my hands lifted up and

God did just that. God, you are worthy to be praised. Brokenness had me in a whirlwind but through my brokenness God brought me back to that place where it was just me and Jesus. My brokenness made me stronger, wiser, and so much better. Hallelujah! I am reminded that Psalm 34:18 (NIV) says, *"The LORD is close to the brokenhearted and saves those who are crushed in spirit."*

KAREN HAWKINS JACKSON

My husband and I are the marriage counselors and provide Christian counseling to those in need. I completed my Doctoral Degree, Ph.D. in Education and started my consulting business. I am a certified holistic life coach, job and career coach, and business consultant, and I am writing my first book. I joined the Prayer Club Ministry as the minister over discipleship and I am on the Ordination Board for the Apostolic Prophetic Network.

> GOD HAS DELIVERED ME, SAVED ME, PROVIDED FOR ME, AND PROTECTED ME, AND HE IS FULFILLING HIS PROMISE TO ME. TO GOD BE THE GLORY FOR THE THINGS HE HAS DONE IN MY LIFE.

CHAPTER 11

The Karen Jackson Story

Being the oldest child can be both a blessing and a curse because you are expected to be an example for others, be strong, and do well in spite of any challenges or setbacks you encounter. At the age of 9, I knew I was different from my younger siblings because I did not have the same interest as my siblings. I saw things that others did not see and I heard things that others did not hear. I lived in a back extension of my great grandmother's (father's grandmother) house with my soon to be divorced mother and father, and two younger sisters. We lived in an impoverished community and oftentimes, food and basic necessities were scarce. I shared clothes and shoes with my siblings, and the three of us slept in the same bed. School was a highlight for me because I was able to eat breakfast and lunch and learn new things. Education was not very important to my father's family, but I really loved learning. At the time, my mother had not finished high school. Getting a high school education was never encouraged. My father also did not finish high school, neither did his three sisters or two brothers.

My parents divorced and my mother moved to a neighborhood not very far from my great grandmother's house. When I was 11 years old, my mother met a man who I will call "Black". Black loved to drink and party. I did not like Black because his eyes were always red like fire, he smelled horrible, he was really dark and I could see something behind his eyes that was scary to me. Black wanted my mother all to himself and he never wanted her to do anything for me and my siblings. When my mother would go to the store, Black would stay home. When my mother would leave the house, Black would make me get in the bed and he would climb on top of me and grind so hard that my upper thighs would hurt. My mother drank almost every day and my sisters, and I were often left home alone to take care of ourselves.

Black would intentionally get my mother so intoxicated that she would pass out. When my mother passed out Black would wake me up in the middle of the night and he would put his tongue in my mouth and ears and molest me. I would lay in bed crying and pleading for him to stop and leave me alone. Black would also pull me out of the bed and make me watch him have sex with my mother. He would make me watch him do things to her and make me rub his private part until he ejaculated on the wall. Black molested, fondled, and abused me for months, and no matter how much I cried and screamed, he would not stop. I was always afraid to go home after school because I knew Black was there and he threatened to kill me if I ever said anything to my mother.

One night as I laid in bed feeling numb listening to the loud blues music coming from the living room, Black leaned over me and tried to put his hand in my underwear again. I screamed to the top of my lungs and started crying uncontrollably. Black ran into the bathroom so my mother would not see him. My mother, intoxicated, stumbled into the room and asked me why I was screaming. I told her what he had been doing to me and what he tried to do that night. My mother called Black, he came out of the bathroom and put his arm around her waist. My mother said to him, "Karen said you were touching her and you know if this is true you are gone". For a second, I felt free of all of the shame, pain, and embarrassment that I had been carrying, but that feeling was short lived. Black kissed her on the cheek and said, "Baby you know I wouldn't do anything to hurt your kids". She said alright now, and they walked away together laughing. I was hurt, ashamed, and angry that my mother did not believe me. At that moment, I felt dirty and confused, and I believed that my mother did not care about me because she did not protect me. My sisters did not talk to me much, so because I had no one to talk to, I would write in my journal and that was my way of releasing some of the pain. After that day, Black taunted and teased me every time he saw me, and then one day, my mother broke up with him. Even after the breakup, Black would call the home phone and harass me by saying mean, nasty and perverted things. After that experience, I would always wear clothes that covered my body from head to toe because I still felt so ashamed.

My mother found a church down the street from the house to take me and my sisters. I got baptized when I was 12 ½ years old and I felt like something happened to me. I began to talk to God all the time and I wrote to him in my journal. I would always feel like God was listening to me, although I never heard him say anything to me. I could also feel when God was near me because I would feel so much peace when I was by myself. I loved reading books and writing in my journal. I also noticed that I began to smell peculiar things, odors that were really bad sometimes, but no one else would smell things I smelled. I would also look at people and see things in them that no one else could see. I could see the deeper things that were hidden behind their eyes. I was never afraid, I just did not understand it. I also would feel uneasy around certain people, almost like I could feel their energy or even their pain, but I did not understand why. I enjoyed going to church because it just seemed like a pleasant place to be. I felt like I was growing close to God and learning more about him, then suddenly my mother stopped going to church.

When I was in high school, my friends convinced me to try out for cheerleading. One night I was coming home from a game, and I felt like someone was watching me. I looked behind me and I saw a man coming towards me really fast. I started running and screaming, and he chased me to my house. He tried to come in the front door behind me, but I was able to push the door and lock it. No one was home and the house was completely dark. He pounded on the windows trying to get in. I hid under the bed until I no longer heard any more noise. When I came from under the bed, I looked out of the window and he was gone. I told my mother what happened, but she didn't do anything, not even report it to the police. It wasn't long afterwards that my mother met "Old Black".

Old Black was 10 years older than my mother, darker than "Black, the first guy she dated. He had a smell that wreaked through his pores, and I never felt safe around him. Old Black loved to gamble and he would keep my mother in the casino day and night. Old Black was controlling and my siblings and I were not allowed to do things with my mother without him. Old Black would talk to himself, or so it appeared, and make strange noises with his mouth, but no one else would notice this but me. He loved to watch horror movies and he kept a mask of the devil hidden in the closet. When I would get up in the middle of the night to use the restroom, he would be standing in the dark with fiery eyes, chanting in the mirror. I would roll my eyes at him and tell him that he was an evil man.

Whenever I was home alone, I would see him floating throughout the house, watching me. I soon learned that he was astral projecting himself. I would also see words written in blood on the walls, and words written backwards on the back of shirts that were laid around the room. I would also hear deep strange voices in the house, and I would often feel dark entities surrounding me. When I would try to sleep, I would always feel spirits over me and I would smell them breathing in my face. I would have nightmares of black snakes surrounding the house and being chased by a demon with red eyes who had a face like a wolf. I was afraid to go to sleep, so I would try to stay awake every night. I tried to tell my mother what was happening to me, but she did not believe me.

When I was 17 years old, I started going to church with my grandmother, my mother's mom. One night at an evening church service, we tarried and I was baptized in the Holy Ghost with the evidence of speaking in tongues. I began to pray in the spirit and anoint my room in the house. I would study the word of God daily. I was so hungry to know God I studied everything I could find. I would play my gospel music and anoint the walls in my room. Old Black did not like me playing gospel music so he broke my radio. I begin to have really bad headaches on one side of my head and the headaches would last for four days at a time. I was later diagnosed with migraine headaches. The headaches were so frequent and I was unable to see, think, eat, or sleep for days at a time. The migraines lasted for years and God delivered me.

I graduated high school as an honors student and I was in the top 10 of my class. After high school, I enrolled in a local university. One day I borrowed Old Black's car to go to school and the brakes went out in the car. I was driving on the highway and could not stop the car. I prayed to God to help me because I no longer had control of the car. I believe that it was an angel that navigated the car to the side of the road and stopped the car. I was so fearful that I would crash and hurt someone or myself, but God sent an angel to help me. Months later, I used Old Black's car again and this time the steering wheel locked as I entered the highway to merge into traffic. I could not steer and I screamed because I realized that it was happening yet again. Once again, I prayed to God to help me and he sent another angel to help me.

I got married when I was 23 years old, and my husband was a womanizer and he was verbally abusive. We lived with my mother and Old Black because we could not afford to live on our own. One day, Old Black stood in my face and said "I need you out of my house". I realized that my light could not dwell in his darkness. I dropped out of school and worked three jobs to save enough money for us to move out, because my husband did not work. I would eat sandwiches every day because that was all I could afford. Late one night I was coming home from work on the bus and the driver, who was running late, would not let me off the bus. I pleaded with him to let me off and he swung the doors open and told me to get off. When I stepped off the bus, he turned the corner and I fell under the bus and the bus rolled over me. That night at the hospital, I was told I did not have any broken bones and I was lucky. The doctor also said "good news, you're pregnant". I was happy about the baby but also sad because I didn't know how I would raise a child by myself. At that time, my husband would not come home for days at a time. I had my son and six months later I paid a friend to take care of my son so I could go back to work. My husband and I would argue all the time and one day he put a knife to my throat and forced me to give him my son's childcare money. I was able to save enough money to buy a car for me and my son, and my husband stole my car. The car was found abandoned and destroyed. I cried out to God to help me get out of this situation.

After five years of emotional, mental, and psychological abuse, I divorced my husband. I enrolled in a university for working adults and found a new church home. My son and I attended church faithfully and I volunteered in different ministries. I began to grow in the knowledge of God and gain an understanding of spiritual gifts. I attended conferences and church events because I wanted to absorb all the knowledge I could obtain about God. I became stronger and bolder in God and my giftings were revealed. It was also revealed to me that I was a Seer, a Prophet who God reveals things to by sight. The Holy Spirit would teach me about my giftings and give me great revelation of scripture. God would speak to me in dreams and visions, and through the discerning of spirits, which operated through my senses (my sight, smell, taste, hearing, and touch). God would reveal intimate details (word of knowledge) about people so I would know how to help them. I learned about spiritual warfare and I would teach others how to pray and intercede for their families.

Six years later, I married my current husband and I moved an hour away from my mother. God had sent me a very loving and compassionate husband to take care of me and support me in the things of God. He encouraged me to go back to school and I graduated from college with my bachelor's degree. I also pursued my master's degree in organizational management. While I was working on my Master's degree, we found out we were expecting. My husband suggested that I stay home during the pregnancy and he took care of me until I had my daughter. We joined another church together and my husband was ordained as a Deacon and I was ordained as a Deaconess. We were also leaders in the intercessory prayer ministry. During this time, I encountered demonic attacks by witches and my mother's husband "Old Black", who was a warlock (revealed to me later) tried to attack my health. God would always show me where the attacks were coming from and I would do spiritual warfare to dismantle the attacks. I completed the Master's in Organizational Management degree and I completed a Master's of Business Administration degree. During this time my family on my father's side would mock me and say mean things against me because I earned degrees and made a better living for myself. At this time, I was also chased on two different occasions by men who tried to attack me going to work and coming home from work, but God protected me from the attacks of the enemy.

God led us to another church and at this church, God called me to be an Evangelist. I was licensed and ordained as an Evangelist.

I also begin working on my doctoral degree. At the present, I preach the good news, teach the word of God, set the captives and the oppressed free, and proclaim the year of God's favor to everyone through small group bible studies and outreach.

DR. EVANGELIST TAMIKE BROWN ————————

Dr. Evangelist Tamike Brown was born and raised in Cordele Georgia to the late Mrs. Maggie Odom Wilkins. She currently resides in Atlanta Georgia. She is the Founder, CEO, President, & Editor of God Anointed Fire Vessels Television Network, TKKJ Video & Audio Production Company (DYWT, LLC), Outreach International Foundation Ministry, Tamike Brown Ministries, Salvation With Fire® Television Broadcast, and Salvation With Fire® Radio Talk Show Host in Atlanta, Georgia.

" BIRTH OUT OF THE FIRE
WHO IS GOD HIMSELF! "

CHAPTER 12
Birth Out of the Fire

As a young teenager and throughout my adult years I went through many different challenges in life. Things that left me broken and torn. I didn't understand all the things I went through or even the reason why at the time. I was brought up in the church as a little girl but had no relationship with God. I had no word knowledge of the Bible, like many of us as teenagers. As a result, my life was in a spiral and took many turns in life that wasn't for my good. I went from being disappointed, discouraged, very un-happy, crying all the time, divorces, abortion, misunderstood, misjudged, misused, physical abuse, falsely accused, in jail, murder mindset, bankrupt, fear, low self-esteem, families and friend's betrayal, persecuted, homeless, and the list goes on and on. Surprisingly, yes I was that girl hiding all those things within. I thought maybe if I hide all those things I would automatically be healed. I was wrong. It only made things worse.

I was living a life on the run. Running to get away from everybody and everything that was troubling me or felt like trouble. I cared nothing for trouble. You mention trouble. I'm out. I was this quiet and shy person but so troubled and torn on the inside. Many times I felt like I was all alone with no one to talk to, so I wanted to vanish and disappear where no one could ever find me. I guess I had my daddy's spirit of running, after he left my sister and I at a young age. He was running from persecutions and left everybody for good. No one ever knew where he was until recently reported, dead, after almost nearly fifty years of no contact with my sister and I and not knowing where he could be found. That's another interesting story all by itself.

At the age of seventeen not only did I hear God's voice but He appeared to me in my bedroom and He was calling me to Himself. I still remember it so clearly as of today. As mentioned, I wasn't knowledgeable of the Word of God but yet within I knew it was God calling me. I didn't understand why He was calling me. I wasn't taught God had a plan and purpose for my life and so forth, and that one day He would call me out of Himself, so when He called and appeared to me I rejected the call. I still wanted to do my thing. I wanted to have fun. I wanted to fit in. I wanted everyone to like me. I wanted to be accepted by people who I thought loved me to include families and friends. I wanted to continue to go to the clubs every now and then. I thought that was "the good life". I went through all these different turns in my life and yet God was calling me but I didn't understand why. When you refuse the call of God He will allow you to go through the burning fire. Why? So you can answer the Call. Throughout my troublesome years, instead of me running to God I thought the answer was in other people. I never gave thought that my answers would be in God when I submit to His *plan* and *purpose* for my life. My joy, happiness, peace, love, and so forth was in God. God was constantly calling me but I kept running. Not only was I running from the Call of God, it got to a point where I was running for my life. Even with me running for my life I still would hear that still small voice and yet I refused the voice. It was like His visitation to me at a young age stayed to the forefront of my mind but yet I was still running.

I started clubbing more often, and the only thing I really enjoyed about the club is that I had the opportunity to dance. I like dancing and I still do to this day. However, now I'm on fire dancing for the Lord. But yes, I thought I was the best dancer on the dance floor and I was stiff as a robot, but you couldn't tell me that (smile). At times I would go to the club with friends but I never smoked or drank alcohol of any kind. I would buy a Coca Cola drink and pour it in my glass to make it look like I was drinking a mixed alcohol drink, you know trying to fit in. One particular night I was asked to dance. After dancing I returned to my seat to drink my coke and someone had poured hard liquor in my cup without me knowing. As I began to drink my coke it burnt my throat (I didn't know anything about sipping). Friends thought it was funny as they did it as a joke however, I didn't see it as a joke at all. It took years for me to recover from a burnt throat. It affected my vocal cords for years.

So, even afterwards I went to the club once more and I began to feel in-different. I felt miserable. I thought the club was the most boring place anyone would want to go. I begin to experience no joy whatsoever. I felt like something wasn't right, but I wanted to give this club thing one more shot to see if I could find happiness. I was not looking for a man, I just wanted to be happy. So, I went one more time and only stayed ten minutes and that was the last time. I said this is not for me. I said God is calling me to Himself. Yes Lord, here I am. This is not the life I want. I'm not happy. Although I said yes, I didn't surrender completely to the Lord like I should have. As I mentioned, when trouble would arise, I would run because that was the only thing I knew how to do. I didn't like trouble at all and neither wanted to be around anyone that was a troublemaker.

Then one day, after experiencing heartbreak after heartbreak, after heartbreak I thought if I started drinking alcohol that my problems would go away. I went and bought this big glass jug of liquor called Gin. I think if you are from the country you call it fifty liquor or something like that. I did buy it not knowing what I was doing because as I said before I was never a person that smoked or drank alcohol of any kind. I took one sip and as I began to take the second sip the Lord stopped me in my trap. He said, "ENOUGH is ENOUGH". Enough was enough and I only had one sip (smile)? When are you going to stop running from me", Father says? At that moment I cried out with a loud cry to God like never before. I threw the whole jug across a concrete area as far as I could in broad daylight and the glass breaking got the people's attention, but yet not one soul asked any questions about the reason for the breaking. I was under God's protective covering as He was breaking me. At that point my life changed forever. I said I surrender all again. This time I gave God a real complete Yes. I stopped running. I said HERE I AM LORD, I AM YOURS, I SURRENDER ALL I gave Him a complete yes. No longer would I run from my troubles. Lord I'm running to You. God said now that I finally got your attention I now have to build you up in me for the Call so I can birth you out of Me. I'm going to birth you out of the Fire because I Am the Fire. I'm going to birth you out of myself so I can "birth myself" through you. I've called you to the Nations.

To fast forward, now God is getting ready to birth me through the fire, which I thought I was already coming out of the Fire. When God said I have to build you up in me, I didn't know building up would require me to go through many fire tests, and many of those fire tests came through family members and friends (mainly family members). Those that you loved the most. Those that were near and dear to you. Those that you were close to. Great persecutions come from family. I've seen many things done and heard things said, however, I pretended I didn't see or hear it and neither thought to vocalize it.

It was like everyone was coming against me. At that time I didn't understand why God was using them to build me up in Him. It was like the Joseph experiences. Joseph's whole family came against him. God set it up that way because Joseph had a Divine Calling on his life. Joseph was chosen by God from the foundation of the world to help his family. A "Divine Calling" many times requires separation so God's Will can be accomplished in the earth. God will allow the separation because it becomes a distraction to His Will. God is not going to allow nothing or anyone to distract His Will for your life when you have given Him a complete yes. You become God's Property. On that note, when it's a "Divine Calling" God will orchestrate every step of the way. He knows what the blueprint looks like as He's the designer. He knows how to get you there. In saying yes to the Will of the Father you will be purified, cleansed, and refined by the Fire. You're being birthed out of God Himself. You will come out looking like fire because the Fire within you will burn "Hotter" than the Fire around you so you'll be able to stay focused to complete the Will of God for your life.

I remember God telling me later in the year 2020, "Do not attach yourself to anyone". He said it three times. As I moved forth in 2021 I truly understood why He said what He said. Not to say I can't talk to anyone or have friends, however, not to become attached because when God is ready to take me to the next level in Him those that I'm attached to will not understand the move of God in my life. Understand, the next move of God has nothing to do with self, it's about His Will being accomplished on the earth. Therefore, God will allow the separation until the mission is accomplished. If you don't understand the mission you won't understand the Will. God will separate you from the distractions. Why? Because you will begin to start pleasing people versus pleasing God.

I remember someone saying to me when God begins to take you higher in Him there will be people that will drop off, and that is the truth. My spiritual eyes were open to see a lot of things. Where God is taking me, some of my family members are not going to understand. Some of my friends are not going to understand. Why? Because of their thinking process. I've been mis-judged by many of them, if not all of them, because they don't understand the call of God on my life. I remember God telling me that He was calling me out and that I can no longer fix it. He said there's no room for expansion trying to fix it if you become stuck. Spending time in God's presence will give you the strength to endure the fire tests. God will allow all the tests to come through families, friends, loved ones, jobs, church people, etc., because He's building you up in Him for a greater call that will benefit mankind. My life is truly nothing without His Presence. I crave His Presence. As I'm being birthed out of the Fire of God, He allows me to see above the trap of my enemies and critics. a good thing to thank God for because it saves you from the disappointments where you're not worrying, stressed, or even mad about what happened and why it happened. It saves you from losing sight of the vision. Nothing surprises you anymore. Your Spirit becomes keen and discerning.

I remember Katherine Kuhlman saying she couldn't count the number of people on one hand that she could call real true friends, they all began to turn their back on her as she began to move higher in God. She began to obey God and not do what her critics thought she should be doing, just like they did Christ. As long as you continue to do what you think your friends want, it cripples God's Plan for your life. When you start worrying about all those things you lose sight of the vision. You lose sight as to why God called you. The ones you thought would be with you through it all end up separating from you. and God will allow the separation. Why? Their assignment was only short term. Some will no longer see you as their friend but will now see you as "she thinks she's all that". They might even say, "he thinks she's better than anyone else, out of all these people why did He choose her". People will congratulate you one moment then the next minute they can't stand you. I've seen a lot, and just because you see a lot doesn't mean you have to vocalize everything you see. That's a distraction. Even through all of that you still have to keep going because the Fire within burns hotter than fire around you. You're being birthed out of the FIRE Who is God Himself.

God said to me three times and I shared it with others. He said when you learn how not to respond to your critics you are now ready for the next level in me. He said, you are finally walking with me, and when you begin to walk with the Lord that's a marvelous thing. He's going to give you His ears, He's going to give you His eyes, and His Divine Power will begin to start operating in your life, because you are finally walking with God, and to walk with God signifies maturity. You can now handle the next level as the next level comes with more persecutions. Birth Out of The Fire who is God Himself!

Spoiler Alert: The book is coming soon!

DAVID WOODS BAYSAH

David Woods Baysah is the pastor of the Tower of
Faith Church of God in Liberia with over 650 members.
He is married to Dr. Maima Baysah, a medical doctor
and a specialized pediatrician.
They have four children.

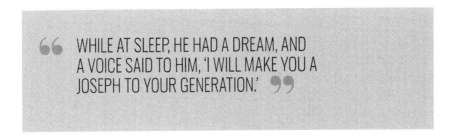

WHILE AT SLEEP, HE HAD A DREAM, AND
A VOICE SAID TO HIM, 'I WILL MAKE YOU A
JOSEPH TO YOUR GENERATION.'

CHAPTER 13

A Journey of Faith

A JOURNEY OF FAITH AND TESTIMONIES: GOD KEPT HIM.

Born in Zorzor District, Lofa County in Liberia, West Africa, one of seven political districts in the northwestern corner of the country. Lofa is the third largest county in Liberia and has three important mountains: Wologisie, Wutizi and Wanigisi.

David was born asthmatic, with many sleepless nights in the hospital with his mom and grandmother by his side. His grandmother was a devoted believer in Christ and kept her faith till death. There were some gloomy days of illness, but God kept him.

He faced many limitations growing up as a child, including going through a brutal 14-year civil war in his country, Liberia. Fleeing the conflict for a year and becoming a refugee in Sierra Leone with his family, he narrowly escaped death fleeing from rebels in Sierra Leone while crossing on a ferry in a place called Potorou. He returned with his family in 1991 to his country after fleeing another civil war in Sierra Leone and back into a civil war that was ongoing.

His family lost everything including savings in banks and returned to a vandalized home with no roof which resulted in him becoming a street peddler at age 13, like many other children during that era. He sold plastic bags, papers and biscuits in the famous Duala market located on Bushrod Island, a densely populated suburb in Montserrado County, Liberia. This was the beginning of the beginning. David went on to sell anything his hands could find, and as the economy worsened, life got harder and unbearable. His mother's desire to see her children become educated was uncompromising and it was unacceptable to not go to school. David came to know the Lord at age 14, and this newfound faith would increase his pain, but his faith in God and assurance that God was faithful no matter what, kept him going. Following his decision to follow Jesus, he refused to do many things he found conflicting with his faith, and this led to many conflicts with his mother and sister. David's faith in God kept him going, and he continued selling anything his hands could find to support himself in school and provide some of his basic needs. With consistency and perseverance, in 1992, his mother and older sister came to know the Lord and they are all serving the Lord today in the same church.

David went on to continue his education and attended one of the premier high schools in Liberia, the Bravid Washington Harris (B.W. Harris) Episcopal High School, by faith. His parents could not afford said school as it was the school some of the President, parliament members, and ministers' children attended. David was daring, and this was one time he saw the tears of his mother as she felt that he would not continue his education due to the cost. She cried and begged him to not consider said school. His father told him to abandon his quest as he could not afford the school of the rich. David went on to work at every construction site he could find, cut flowers and grass for families, and spent days on the Du River fishing for fish to sell. In a month, David was able to generate his first semester school fees and he started school. When his father saw that he was serious, and would not give up, he decided to support his education at the prestigious high school. To attend this school, David had to relocate from home. Reverend Charles Summerville, a minister of the Church of God in Liberia and his wife Jamba Gray Summerville, were gracious enough to accommodate David in their home. He stayed with the Summerville's until he completed high school. Prior to this phase of his life, his mother went blind for two years, and at that point, is when David first decided that he would commit suicide. In the meantime, he knew he had to step up. He would go to school and leave after school to sell anything his hands could find down at the waterside, a major market center in the heart of Monrovia, the capital city of Liberia. He would walk distances selling and would get home by night, then his older sister and himself would cook food for the family. "My youth was stolen, and I never experienced the joy of youthfulness" said David. In his pain and anguish, he decided again that he would commit suicide. He mentally prepared himself for two weeks leading up tothe week he decided would be when he would commit suicide. He was moody and avoided everyone close to him, including his mother and sister. He took pills to make him feel no pain and took a knife into his room and locked his door. As he pulled the knife, something happened that cannot be explained up to this day. He became so weak that he could not lift the knife and he broke down and cried himself to sleep. While at sleep, he had a dream, and a voice said to him, "I will make you a Joseph to your generation". He woke up with a new vigor for life, and until this day, he has never lost hope.

He lost his father (Henry Baysah) during his first semester at the University of Liberia. Life became unbearable for David. He applied for a scholarship through his church to study in the Republic of Ghana. He was informed that he was selected but a few days after, his name was replaced, until today he does not know why? He was devastated, broken, and hurting inside. His high school friend who had traveled to the USA while they were still in high school, filled in for David. All his immigration papers were set and ready, but there was something that David could not explain about rejecting the offer. He said, "I knew God had a plan for me in Liberia, and my location could not limit God from working," so David turned down the process and the rest of them left for the USA. David would only get to meet his friend after 19 years in New York City. David called his friend "Kaifa Kanneh" his brother.

Almost everyone his father mentioned that he helped to get an education, could not help him, even after multiple visits and requests for assistance. He sought help from friends and continued doing what he knew best "selling" to continue his education. While supporting himself, there were constant outbreaks of clashes between warring factions which led to abrupt closure of schools most of the time. It took him almost seven years to complete his first bachelor's degree. During this period, a family friend, Mr. Monroe D. Parker got in touch with him from the USA and decided to help him. Based on this, he later enrolled at another university, the African Methodist Episcopal University, and was attending both universities at the same time taking about 40 credits each semester and still making 3.5 to 4.00 points GPA. With two bachelor's degrees, David received tuition assistance from one of his professors, Reverend Dr. Herman Browne, an Episcopal minister of the gospel who would become an academic mentor to David which led him to enroll in his first master's program. With admission into graduate school, David started applying to be a teacher, and his application to one of his previous schools was rejected. He later applied to one of the universities he graduated from to serve as a teaching assistant, and he was denied and told to find something meaningful to do with his life. David was again daring and would not give up. He contacted a former professor, Professor Sekou Konneh, who agreed to mentor him as a university lecturer, and after a year, David had the opportunity to be employed at the university that rejected him previously. At 27, David was lecturing Introduction to Sociology. At the age of 29, David became the chairperson of his department and became a sought-out sociologist nationally. After four years, David needed a new challenge, and he went on to serve as Deputy Program Coordinator of a World Bank funded project in the health sector of Liberia and it was through this medium David and his wife purchased their farmland, that is now called "ADARA Farms". They are producing palm oil, rubber-latex, guava leaves for tea, and animal husbandry.

David has gone on to work with his church, Church of God, in Liberia. He has worked on several World Bank funded projects, worked with UNICEF across Rwanda, Madagascar, Ethiopia, Mozambique, Lesotho, Zambia, South Sudan, Angola and other places analyzing education systems and developing sector plans. He has worked with several institutions and traveled to over 30 countries across four continents. Today, David at age 42, is the Founder and Leader of the ADARA Group, comprising the ADARA Research and Management Consultancy, ADARA Farms, and the ADARA University. The latter is expected to open in 2022 with infrastructure works 90% complete. David has impacted many lives and continues to impact nations, people, and communities. Two of his major initiatives are "sponsorship for underprivileged kids to access education" which has seen over 100 children and adults across pre-primary, primary, secondary, and universities, and "Pads for Girls in Schools" an initiative he supports with the "Foundation for the Advancement of Girls" as the lead agency. Today, David and his wife Maima Baysah have over 25 persons employed and are planning to increase employment to 200 with the opening of ADARA University in 2022. It has been a journey of faith. He is also currently the pastor of the Tower of Faith Church of God in Liberia with over 650 members, and is married to Dr. Maima Baysah, a medical doctor and a specialized pediatrician with four children. This journey of faith has taught him several lessons:

1. God has a plan for everyone irrespective of your condition, creed, background, or the color of your skin, **DO NOT** give up.
2. Never make a permanent decision based on temporary situations, the situation is just a chapter in your life, and not the last chapter, **DO NOT** give up.
3. Your ideas and dreams can influence and impact your world, do not cast them away, keep hope alive and persevere, **DO NOT** give up.
4. In every limitation, there lies a testimony, do not allow your limitations to limit you, limit them and declare your testimony, **DO NOT** give up.
5. When the going gets tough, let your faith get tough, with God, all things are possible, **DO NOT** give up.

6. Never limit your dreams to the size of your pockets, think beyond your background, bank account, and condition, **DO NOT** give up.
7. Seek God in all you do and all you do will submit to God's will.

JOSEPH NIMELY

Hebrew 11:6, *"God rewards those that diligently seek him."*

> 66 WHATEVER YOU FIND TO DO, DO IT WITH ALL YOUR MIGHT, CAUSE GOD IS WATCHING OUR HEARTS AND MOTIVES...IF GOD CAN RAISE ME FROM POVERTY TO THE PROMISE. HE CAN DO THE SAME FOR YOU. DON'T GIVE UP. HOPE IS ON THE WAY. 99

CHAPTER 14

Processed for the Promise

I am Joseph Tweh Nimely, Sr. My parents are Henry W. Nimely and Beatrice Weah. I was born July 3, 1990. I am the last of 17 children both from my father and mother. I grew up in the interior of Grand Kru County. I am from a very poor family. Nobody in my family has ever owned a bike, before a car, nor has anyone built their own house. I am the first to marry, graduate with a degree. Growing up as a child I never saw electricity, good health facilities, cars etc...I didn't have the time to eat good food. We ate from the bushes and drank from the creeks, interestingly we were drinking from the same creek we washed and bathed in. My parents were not educated, so we lived a very low life. Later I came to Monrovia at age 10 and when I arrived here, I moved in with my aunt. The house I saw was no different from the palm tree hut I lived in. I remembered my aunt would go to the beach and bring fish. We would dry it at night and sell it in the morning. After everything, we ate only one time at night. Later I started fishing for fish and frogs that I would sell to help my house and my aunt. I would walk from swamp to swamp catching frogs from morning till evening. At night I would set baskets to catch also. I remembered getting sick and my aunt and grandma didn't have money to take me to hospital, so they just left me and observed. God used O.R.S to revive me. I came from the village, where we are used to farming and cutting down trees and I remembered my mom telling me that I was to die in a canoe that capsized and it was God who delivered me. She said, "Amongst my brethren I am the light".

I started going to school and my lunch was ten dollars a day. I would walk fifteen to thirty minutes to school every day. My father would climb palm trees to earn a living and also support me. I later moved in with my sister and her husband and it was hell. Writing can't explain it. I would wake up as early as 5 am, fetch water at the handpump, clean the dishes and then make breakfast and hot water. After all this I would walk to school. After school, I would go straight to the market and then home to cook. By the time I was done, I would clean my little sister up. I would then grab my kerosine, fuel oil, matches, candles and mosquito coils to sell and would walk around until 8 pm. When I would reach back home it was back to work. My aunt's husband, who's late now, used to work with President Tolbert's son as a security man. He would sometimes collect the remaining food from the tables of his bosses and children and would bring it to us and it was the best food we all would wait for, because it had chicken and was prepared. Whether it was balanced food we didn't care. This was my life until my sister's husband accused me of stealing money. I was treated like a criminal, tortured, and taken to the police cell. I knew at that moment my parents couldn't help. All they wanted was for me to go to school. I cried and asked God why, and then I was punished from 6pm-10pm. I got sick and at this was the point I started developing my music passion.

The worst of all is that I lived as an orphan. No father's love and no mother's care...I was making my life by myself. I moved out when I was in eleventh grade. When I moved out I was paying my own school fees and my father started to assist me. By this time I was put out for Waec Fees. It was the same day I was sitting in the compound of the school, thinking of what to do, that I received a call that "your dad is dead" I was so confused. That was 2010 and after that life was so hard for me...it was tough. I was tempted to join lots of crazy things. I had been sleeping from one friend's place to another.

In 2011, I moved with a friend who I connected with through music and I started playing and teaching the choir. They would give me 75ld per practice day. One time I went home and cried. The pastor called me up one time and asked people to give me some used clothes because I would wear my kittle sandals and a white round neck shirt every Sunday, until they named me Michael Jackson. I was renting a room for ten dollars (USD) and I couldn't pay. Six months was $60 USD and it was too much. I have taken other children to stay with me, cause I am a people person and the landlord gave me a notice. I couldn't pay but I couldn't leave. Where would I go? So she took me to court and the sheriff came. I left that night and went to a girl's house. I moved with my things that night to that girl's house. We were all in one room. At midnight when I am tired, she comes with a visitor and I am forced to be outside until she's done. looking at all this I didn't see anything. At a radio station in Liberia, the manager invited me there. He heard me sing and wanted to promote me, but the option was to do secular music. Looking at my background and my life at the time, the opportunity crossed my mind. I refused and he threw me out. I would be so hungry that I'd buy coconut and cassava and eat it for the whole day, or maybe eat just cornmeal with sugar in it. Sometimes when I was broke, I would go to the tea shop to wait for the empty milk cup, to at least give my tea a taste. Every church I went to I served with my ALL. Not on salary. I would walk from church-to-church teaching choirs, just to eat. I got the call that God was calling me to be a pastor and I wanted to escape or cancel the call. This strange (that's what I thought at the time) lady that I met for the first time, somewhere far from my home, explained my life to me and told me God had called me to preach his word and he's taking my ministry around like Sonnie Badu. Those were her words. From there straight away I entered the seminary and acquired my BTH, Bachelor's of Theology. By the grace of God. I didn't have money and no one wanted a pastor in their office.

I got married and grew worse. My wife and I would sleep starving many nights and I'll look at her and ask God why? I didn't have any money to send my wife to school or and to even take care of my house rentals. But it was God. One morning I was home resting cause I just came from tarry and my landlord came and disgrace me for his rent. My wife was so embarrassed. I went to the bathroom and God said to me, "it's the process." I am asking Him and he tells me that "because you're not seeing me, doesn't mean I am not with you." My faith was attacked because I felt that God was sleeping or had forgotten my case. Meanwhile, prophets and prophetess have spoken over my life that God said to them he'll take me from nations to nations teaching His word through songs and through preaching; yet I didn't see any way possible.

I have been tested, hungered, betrayed, rejected, etc...but I knew God would pick me up. If He can raise me up from my bad situation, it's possible for you. My entire life has been painful. I suffered at the hands of landlords. I was thrown out many times. I was thrown out with my wife and kid. I looked at my wife and kid and tears flowed from my eyes at a certain point. It felt like the world was on my shoulders. Although I was struggling, my mom was in the village and asked me to support her. My siblings looked to me for help. All my big sisters and brothers were begging me for clothes, meanwhile my friend and I had one coat suit. I was the first person to wake up in the morning every Sunday wearing the coat. I took some really big coats from a friend and carried them to the tailoring shop to resize them. The guy didn't do a good job and I still wore the clothes that were too big. I couldn't afford to have them altered for a second time. When in 7th grade, I used to go to the dumpsite to look for empty bottles and sell them for lunch money. After high school, I went to the Liberia Dujar Technical College to study Nursing. All my friends that I was living with, parents gave them their school fees. I still had to register. When we made it to the campus, I went with them to the admission office. The lady who registered them, when it came to me, asked me for my letter from my dad. I told her my dad is dead and my mom was in the village. Even if she was here, she's not lettered. She left and went into the president's office, not knowing it was the pastor of the choir I was teaching and he put me on his walls. I was registered. I started school and walked to school everyday. It was about forty five minutes away, going and coming. I would be hungry all day. Going back to my family's house was a challenge, because when it rained, whether you were inside or outside...the house leaked and there was no cement on the floor.

During those times, it was difficult to afford clothes. I didn't have any. I would borrow clothes to attend programs and return the clothes the next day. I couldn't understand my life and myself; I didn't know where I was heading. "Every time God calls you to His promise, there's always an Era called 'Process' that God takes you through to know your heart and to keep you humble." One day I was in the bathroom, talking to myself, saying out loud that I must do something. I felt the need to try and travel to get money, but God told me that night, that *"I am the one who calls you and has promised to take you to the nations of the world"*. God is always right. He's always on time. I realized, a "poverty mindset" isn't good at all, it limits your thinking. It makes you feel inferior, like a beggar. Since I changed my mindset and started getting involved into the things of God, my life has taken a different meaning. I worked hard to get to where I am. I slept in darkness from 1990-2011, before I started seeing the current activity changing in my life. It was by God's grace that I came in contact with my spiritual father, a man that God brought into my life at my darkest hour. His teachings changed my thoughts and taught me how to wait upon the Lord. He explained his life story to me and I was motivated looking at his success and hearing a very ugly story. Since then he has been a blessing to my family and I both physically and spirituality.

Fast forward. It was the week of the church convention. My wife was so discouraged and she said to me babe, "It seems like God is not hearing us even though we are faithful to him." I took that as a challenge and chose not to miss the convention. I was so glad I was obedient to God's leading and attended. It was then that God showed up through Prophetess Shanika Stewart who decided to actualize the promises of God in my life. I pray to support as many young and old people with the same issues as mine, because I know what God told me. They are my priorities. God bless you Prophetess Shanika Stewart for re-writing my story and for God using you to establish His promise. A special thanks to my wife, the most patient and loving woman on earth. Babe, you loved me unconditionally and I owe you my all. My junior boy, I bore you when I had nothing and you're partaker of my crisis. I love you and I owe you everything. Thanks to my parents Bishop and Mother John Kun Kun and the City of Light family for your prayers and support. My wonderful in-laws Reverend and Pastor Francis F.B Tamba...thank you.

In life, always serve the Lord from your heart. Hebrew 11:6 (KJV) says, "God rewards those that diligently seek him". Whatever you find to do, do it with all your might, because God is watching our hearts and motives. If God can raise me from **Poverty To The Promise,** He can do the same for you. Don't give up. Hope is on the way.

By Joseph Nimely

BISHOP JACOB HENRY HARRIS

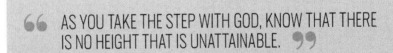

66 AS YOU TAKE THE STEP WITH GOD, KNOW THAT THERE IS NO HEIGHT THAT IS UNATTAINABLE. 99

—*Bishop Jacob Henry Harris*

CHAPTER 15

The Greater Power

BISHOP JACOB HENRY HARRIS IS A LIBERIAN AND A PASSIONATE LOVER OF THE LORD JESUS CHRIST.

He was born on December 25, 1963 in upper Fendell, Louisiana, Liberia to the union of Mr. Sengbeh Jorkour Bowen and Mrs. Yatta Kula Bowen. Bishop Harris' biological parents were illiterate, but they endeavored never to allow their son to thread that same path. Mr. and Mrs. Bowen quickly supported little Jacob to go to school like other school kids in the country. Unfortunately for small Jacob Harris, his father died when he was at a tender age. This had a huge impact on his upbringing. His mother who didn't have education had to now be the breadwinner for the family. She remarried to Mr. Alexander Harris. His new father was an educated man who gave him every opportunity to pursue his primary and secondary education. Jacob now took the last name of his stepfather, Mr. Alexander Harris. It is a name he has used all through his life.

Bishop Jacob H. Harris had the passion and determination to complete secondary school. He enrolled at the most popular government run secondary school in the entire Bomi County, C.H. Dewey Central High School located in the county's capital, Tubmanburg. He stayed there until completing high school in

1982. Young Jacob Harris was also athletic and talented. He played sports in secondary school, he was also a goal keeper as a soccer player. He played even in the National counties sport meet, a tournament played to find a yearly winner amongst the 15 counties in Liberia in different sports (Basketball, Kickball and Football). He represented Bomi County in the football team in the year 1978.

After high school, Jacob Harris relocated to Monrovia, the nation's capital in pursuit of better living. He was hungry for success and wanting to always stand out as the one who will break the lifestyle of poverty and mediocrity in his family. Jacob came to Monrovia in 1983. Jacob had a terrible background spiritually. He worshiped other gods; he was made to join the poro society (a traditional society for boys) early as a young man. He rose to be the (Kpana) a rank of chief in that demonic order. When he came to Monrovia and was pursuing a betterment of life, God was also intentional about young Jacob Harris. Jacob met the Lord Jesus Christ in a Sunday worship service at the Eliza Turner A.M.E Church in 1985. God used the sermon of Rev. J.E. January to hook young Jacob's heart and bring him to salvation. He accepted Jesus and from that day forward, he has never been the same.

Now as a Christian, Jacob's direction for success, defined as financial stability and economic liberation of his family were changed to living a God pleasing life. All he wanted now was to please God. His pursuit of God, as God himself led him to a Bible believing Church, headquarter Church of God. His pursuit of God caused him to enroll at the Church of God Bible School (Liberia Bible Institute) in 1986. In his secondary year, the call of God was seen by the National Overseer of the Church of God

Bishop J. A. Williams. He was appointed to continue a fellowship in Gardnerville, Stephen A. Tolbert Estate – an outline of the nation's capital Monrovia. That fellowship grew into a Church, and he became the first Pastor of that church, Tower of Faith, Church of God. He pastored that church for over 23 years of his life. In that place, God used him mightily to raise men and women for effective ministry. He now has sons and daughters who are Bishops, Pastors and Apostles.

In the active service to God and the people he led in that local church, he found his soulmate Reverend Jessena Grant Harris. They got married on April 17, 1999. Bishop Harris loves this woman. He is a man that is never satisfied with being ordinary or following the usual pattern. He found out that there was a need to understand scriptures for what it really is. He enrolled in the Liberia Baptist and Theological Seminary and graduated in 2005 with a Bachelor's Degree in Theology. Bishop Jacob Harris' love for ministry grew more and more. He has a deep desire for lost souls like our Lord Jesus Christ. This passion was what God needed to work with him on the next level of his ministry. Church of God World Missions appointed him as a National Overseer for the church work in a French Islamic dominated nation of Guinea and went on proclaiming Jesus in an uncompromising way. God caused signs and wonders to be revealed by his hands that brought men to their knees. The church grew and many souls were hooked on Jesus. Bishop Jacob H. Harris was assigned in Guinea for ten (10) unbroken years. He was able to raise new ministers and plant new churches to carry the work of Jesus forward.

While serving in Guinea, God had another assignment in the nation of his birth. In September 2020, the leadership of the

Church of God World Missions appointed Bishop Jacob H. Harris again as the new National Overseer in Liberia. The God who carried him through, has never stopped his work in him. Bishop Jacob H. Harris loves and is ready to work for God.

LIFE BEFORE CHRIST

In Galatians 1:15, the Apostle Paul gives a testimony of the dealings of God in his life *"But when it pleased God, who separated me from my mother's womb, and called me by Grace".* This statement shows that God had Paul's life assignment even before his birth. The reason for his birth was to fulfill this very assignment. Mine was no different.

When I sit in today's view and picture my yesterday, I see the devil's plan to make God's purpose a lie in my life. My early childhood experience was terrible. It was one that made me succumb to the traditions and cultural influences of the day. This led me to worshiping an unknown god like the people in Athens. (Acts 17:22-31). I was introduced to a secret men society in our traditional setting called the poro Society. I was told that this was the path that every man born in our county must take to learn to be a real man. Any man who refuses the poro society is seen as an improper man (sinner). In this society, we were marked, blood was taken from us, and we were given strange powers to do things beyond the natural.

I remember back then I used to cut off my tongue and join it again. I rose to the rank of "Kpana" in society. It is a title given to the first Child alive. Like a royal monarch inheriting the throne of his ancestors. I was in line to receive the "Kpana" title. This carries a lot of respect spiritually. Like Paul, looking back, I count it all as a loss for the excellency of Christ. (Phil 3:8-10). All these powers failed me. It couldn't keep me from sickness, death or hell. It gave me fame in my community but intended to take my soul in exchange. Like many young men who had not come to know King Jesus; I also had my share of lust and alcohol. I played soccer and it gave me fame in the county. I was the senior goalkeeper of the county's soccer team. This made the girls flirt over me. I thought this is an experience every young person should desire.

Satan made me look like a King but I was dying in the pool of my destiny. I remembered one day, we went out partying at a local nightclub with my friends and the girls. I had a cigarette pack in my hand partying the night away. Then there was a sudden gun shot. The gun shoot took the cigarette pack from my hand and I never attempted going back to any night club again in my life. God saved me that very day. Isn't this God good? He used the most life-threatening situation to bring me to the place of truth. You might be going through that very life-threatening situation right now; I ask that you open up your heart to know what God is saying. Even though the experience of the gunshot scared me, it didn't change me. Making a decision of change based on an event outside of encountering the very true word of God was just temporary. I continued other bad habits I was involved with. It was not until I met the real change maker, Jesus, that He truly transformed my life.

MEETING JESUS

Growing up knowing the path to a successful life as a man was for poro society, Jesus was the last name to believe in. The devil is very calculative in his dealings. He understood God's plan for my life and planned to abort it. He made me believe the power that could guarantee my success in life was that of the gods of the poro society. I lived for magic and charms. I was blinded by applause and vain praises of men. I could do anything for these magical powers. It was until I met Jesus. After a lifestyle I was so ashamed of, Jesus met me in a Sunday service. I had received an invitation from a cousin to attend and I consented. As the clergyman, Reverend J. E. January preached the undiluted word of truth. This message brought me to my knees asking God to forgive my sins. I surrendered my life that day to a greater power than I was used to. I ask Jesus to now take over my sinful life; and make it what he wants. This brought joy to me. It was one I had never experienced before. I left the service with a new song in my mouth and a new hunger to know the God that was introduced to me in that meeting. Friends and family members couldn't comprehend how traumatic and quick this was. Their friend and brother who chased girls, lust in charms and alcohol would now be talking about God and his word. Meeting God is the best thing that has happened to me. From that day I desired to know this God every day of my life.

MY JOURNEY AS A CHRISTIAN AND CALL INTO MINISTRY

Jesus truly saves, He changed me greatly. He didn't change me to a bench warmer in the Kingdom, he placed a passion in me for ministry. The hand of the Lord led me to a Bible believing church in Paynesville City, Headquarter Church of God. I met men and women who also loved God that helped me quickly. I enrolled at the Church's Bible school to help me understand God's word. It was an essential tool in my life of ministry. I was taught many Christian truths that have guided my life these many years. I cherished these formative years. My passion began so visibly and noticeable that my overseer called me out for an assignment to oversee a fellowship that had been on going to one of the cities outside of Monrovia.

I didn't fully understand what God was doing, but I accepted the call. Sometimes you don't need to fully understand God before saying yes. This is a lesson for every person desiring to do ministry for God. In this call, God taught me His ways. I had to learn how to trust him for any and everything. Some days I went walking over three miles to do evangelism. I did it with joy. I had to sleep in the market buildings; I even remembered that there were days that I went to bed without food. In all this, God was faithful.

The fellowship grew into a church. It was on the ground of intense prayer and evangelism. Ministers, these are the path to making ministry work. Pray, pray and pray. This didn't come without challenges. The church battles spiritually for the space to operate physically with people. We went through some legal battles that landed us to the Supreme Court of Liberia. Looking through the scriptures, I see that period of my life like Nehemiah trying to rebuild the walls of Jerusalem. All in that fight, I saw the hand of God every time. Jesus is faithful.

In the midst of the opposition, we were raising men and women of God for Kingdom advancement. I remember a specific day that my wife and I along with some other members of our congregation had to sleep behind bars at the Monrovia Central prison (the nation's biggest detention center). God used those tough times to teach me to trust him. Ministers (those wanting to serve God), understand the call to whatever service in ministry comes with a price. Be ready to pay your price. By the help of

God, we were able to secure the church land and also raise a church that prayed and read the word of God. I have seen people fighting for titles and positions, my advice is don't fight, go through the process of maturing. When you are mature enough, God will elevate you. I pay my dues, you must too. Jesus said every man picks up his cross and follows him.

WHAT GOD IS DOING?

Through these years, besides the lessons learned, God has been doing wonders. I have watched God heal men from the diseases man labeled incurable. God, through his power, led me to pray for many barren women desiring children, and by his grace we have countless testimonies. Let me share a few miracles; if you yield yourself to trusting God and his power. Remember I have tasted other powers, but what I have seen God do and is still doing are immeasurable. One day, we had an insane person brought to our church. We were led to pray for that person who had spiritual issues that made her mad. We prayed and I called her to be normal, by the grace of God the Almighty, she became normal again. Glory be to God.

We have also seen a nation dominated by Muslims and highly fitchy, come to know Jesus. We saw men surrender their charms and protections around their waist to follow Jesus. God can work through you. You don't have to be any other person than what God has made you. There are people that just want to hear you the way you are. I couldn't imagine in my wildest dream that a boy who used to play with charms and shed blood to other gods can be the one preaching the gospel of Jesus Christ. I, Jacob H. Harris from an unknown background, would be leading a whole nation of God's people. This can only be the power of the Highest God. As you take the step with God, know that there is no height that is unattainable.

CONCLUSION

This is a good exercise to me as a believer, who has the passion for God's ministry and passing all these experiences to my generation. For the sake of young ministers generations after me, I have written what I call a summary of my life and ministry. It would take years to write a complete story. My prayer is that this will bring glory to our Lord and Savior, Jesus Christ and blessings and improvement to many.

By Jacob Harris

PRINCESS DORBOR

Lives in Monrovia, Liberia
Born April 3, 2005
Phebe Gray Orphan
Church of God World Mission
Contact: womenoffaithandhope@mail.com

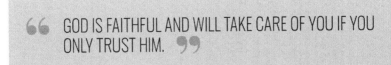

66 GOD IS FAITHFUL AND WILL TAKE CARE OF YOU IF YOU ONLY TRUST HIM. 99

CHAPTER 16

He Protected Me For Purpose

MY LIFE STORY

My name is Princess Dorbor. I was born to Janet Karma and Joe Dorbor in Benson Hospital. During my upcoming years it was not easy for my parents because of financial difficulties. Four years after my primary education from ABC, my parents found it difficult to pay my school fees. When I was in fourth grade, my father suddenly passed away and life became more difficult for my mother to handle alone.

My mother left the interior and she came to capital Monrovia with a sickness where she was taken to the Abundant Life Church of God to meet with the Bishop Mansah who prayed for her and God healed her. There she became a member. At that time I was living in the village. My uncle brought me to Monrovia to live with his wife, where I was going to school. Later I decided to go back to my mother. After my mother came for me, things did not stay okay. Then Bishop Mansah took me to the Gray Orphanage Home to get qualified education.

PRINCESS STORY

It is estimated that over 6,000 children lost either one or both of their parents to Ebola in Liberia in 2014 and 2015. Princess Dorbor was born on April 3, 2005 and lived with both of her parents. However, on April 13, 2018, her father, Mr. Joe Dorbor, died leaving her and a sibling to a single mother who was jobless. This left the family devastated and life became unbearable for the family.

Princess mother Janet Kamara who was left with no option, decided to seek help with the caring and livelihood of the children. The Phebe Gray orphanage was gracious enough to open their doors to both children. Church of God World Mission Liberia owns and operates the Phebe Gray Orphanage home in Liberia. It is located on a main highway near the Roberts International Airport. The orphanage is the host to over 100 orphans from different parts of the Country. Since 2018 when Princess was 13 years old in the 8th grade, Princess and her brother have now been living at the orphanage home.

Princess is now in the 10th grade going to the 11th and aspires to study finance following her high school graduation. According to Princess, "If the orphanage had not opened their doors to us, we would not have been able to continue our education". She is a determined young lady but also is faced with challenges as she is also in need of a tutor to help her with her study and sometimes has very limited out-of-pocket expenses. Princess is active in the church and sings with the church choir.

Princess had a dream of becoming a lawyer or medical doctor. In 2021, Princess met Prophetess Shanika Ann Stewart in Liberia on a mission trip. This trip changed things for Princess.

God really used Prophetess Stewart to pour into her and Princess looked to her as a spiritual mother. Princess is still on her path to greatness, learning a lot at a young age. God is faithful and will take care of you if you only trust Him. Her prayer is that her story will bless others like herself through the sharing of her testimony. My thanks and appreciation goes to her mother Janet Kamara, Bishop Mansah, and her spiritual mother Shanika Ann Stewart. To God be the glory.

TINA ARBUCKLE

> 66 GOD WILL FIND A WAY TO GET TO YOU EVEN SOMETIMES WHEN YOU ARE AT ROCK BOTTOM. 99

CHAPTER 17

From Being Fine to Finding God

There was a time when I did not know God. I went to church every Sunday, singing in the choir but I still did not know who God was. As years went by, I had the mindset that my body and shape would get me what I needed and wanted. At that time, I was struggling to pay bills, living in a housing authority barely making it. It was like I was doing everything inside the church right, ushering, singing in the choir and praying, but on the inside of me there was no God. I had the attitude that since my body is what attracted men, let me see how much money I could get. I talked to this man, so he could pay this bill, talked to him he could pay that bill and so on. I did not look at myself as a prostitute because they weren't strangers to me, and I was thinking they were my boyfriends. It was so crazy. In the midst of me struggling, I lost my car but I still felt like I had it all. I kept telling myself I just needed to find the right man not knowing the right man was God.

I met another man. This one was very special to me. When he came around, I would drop everything. Where I messed up was I gave him the power over me, and he knew it. How many of you all have that one man that you can't see anything beyond him? I knew he wasn't right for me, but if I can be blunt for a minute his sex overpowered everything. Years went by with me being stuck with him not because I loved him, but because I loved the sex. It was like a strong hold on me. What I have learned is that God is a jealous God. I can't worship man and God at the same time. It took years to figure that out. While years were going by things started to change in my life. My body did not look the same any more. So my thought at this point was no "body", minus no man, minus no money, leaves me with nothing.

God will find a way to get to you even when you are at rock bottom. In the year of 2014, I pulled up at work and couldn't get out of the car. I started crying and called out His name and said Lord I need your help. I can't do it without you. It was like a breath of fresh air came over me hearing the Lord say, "I've been, I just needed you to acknowledge me and welcome me in". As I started to seek God first, things started to look clearer to me. Man had me staying comfortable at a low paying job. I could stay on food stamps or with my low income my rent at $180.00 a month, rent and lights included. How can you beat that? Well, I will tell you how you can beat that. Once you put God first, and trust him, and have faith everything will line up right.

I had to think bigger than my situation. I had to work. I wanted more in life. I had to step out on faith and get out of my comfort zone, which was fast food jobs. Sometimes the devil will have you miss out on your blessing only because you are scared to move, scared of change. To be honest I was so scared, but I thank God I made that move. Once making a better income I moved out of public housing as a result of seeking God. Now you might think I had it all together, finally learned my lesson. NOPE. The fastest I would make money I would spend the money, (income tax, unemployment, stimulus check) it was because I still had the mindset of poverty. I painted a pretty picture on the outside, but it didn't reflect my true situation. I'm here to let you know, to get out of poverty you just can't think moving out of the hood will save you. Learn how to use your money wisely. Open saving accounts. and invest in yourself. Get educated on money management. Change your mindset. You can help someone else like I hope this is helping you.

I hope my story falls in the hands of those women who believed that they needed to use their body to get what they wanted, or were scared to strive for better. My story is to let them know that they don't need to depend on man, if they only depend on God. He is our Way Maker. Just like they ask can anything good come out of Nazareth, I'm asking can anything good come out Of the hood? Yes it can because I'm a living witness.

By Tina Arbuckle

MONICA WILLIAMS

> 66 I HAD TO STOP BLAMING MY UPBRINGING FOR MY LIFE TODAY. MY UPBRINGING WAS A GUIDE AND IT WAS IN THE PAST. WE ARE TO PRAY FOR FORGIVENESS OF OTHERS PAST TRANSGRESSIONS AS WELL AS OUR OWN. 99

CHAPTER 18
K.I.S.S

I grew up in a home of Baptist believers in the late sixties. I attended a Baptist church and knew nothing more than the Baptist life. It consisted of going to church from eight or eleven in the morning until four or eight in the evening. From infancy to young adulthood this was all I knew. Sunday mornings we always had to make sure we were dressed in our Sunday meeting's best and were prepared to be gone all day. To me it was just another day of the week where we spent the day listening to the choir sing and a man of God bringing the word.

Now Saturday was a completely different day from Sunday. Every Saturday we, meaning my mom, aunts, cousins, my sister and myself, would get up at seven in the morning and get out into the shopping world. We would start at a huge swap meet, then multiple garage sales and end up in the Garment District in the crowded downtown Los Angeles area. This would last until five in the evening. My uncles would have been fishing in the early morning and then preparing for the fish fry that evening. The entire family and friends would congregate at one family member's house and let the party begin. The Blues music would be blasting in the background along with loud talking and laughter and the alcohol would be plentiful. The fish would be frying in a never-ending delight all night. It was a party until the cows came home. The funny thing is there was never any mention of Jesus or being thankful for what He had provided.

If your household was like mine there was a Bible (and probably a big Bible) laying somewhere in a room that you were never to enter unless it was a special occasion. This Bible was a staple in most households and also collected a lot of dust in those same households. The only time I actually witnessed prayer was when my grandmother would visit us all the way from Alabama. I saw her kneel in the mornings when she awoke and again before going to bed in the evenings. I never knew what she prayed for and I never knew why she did what she did. It was strange to see her old body get down on the floor kneeling to someone I never really knew each day during her visit.

My household only gave Jesus one meal a week and that was all day on Sundays. There was never a time I can remember bringing Jesus into the house other than on Sunday or when there was a death in the family. I just remember living in the world and enjoying a "Jesus free" life. My life consisted of school, parties and church in that order. I felt like I had an easy life full of nothing but fun and finding new ways to enjoy the devil's playground. It was never complicated. It was never hard to live a good simple life. It is what I like to call *simple while being stupid*". I lived my life from a young age of pre teenage years to young adult years being as carefree as life would allow. I never focused on those moments of watching my grandmother praying on her knees. No, I focused more on the life of parties that my family showed me most of my young adult life. Even after all I was doing, I never realized Jesus was there with me the whole time. I later realized that my grandmother was the still small voice in the flesh that I ignored with every visit. She never wavered from her humbled servitude to our Jesus.

"Keeping It Simple Stupid" had been my mantra for most of my life. What I did not realize was that Jesus was and is simple. He is not nor will He ever be complicated. The complication came when I got in the way. The stumblinges came when I got in the way. The troubles came when I got in the way. Jesus was the way but it was me that got in His. I got in the way of Him blessing me. Sometimes we do not realize just how simple Jesus is, how non complicated He is, and how true to His word He is. He is not a man that He would lie (Numbers 23:19). Some of us believe life has to be difficult in order to be blessed or to receive His mercy and grace. We learn to follow Him, to meditate on His word and to lay all of our worries at the cross. However, we tend to lay our worries at the cross and then go back and pick them back up. This is the mindset that makes you believe you can do things faster and better than Jesus can. It is like praying for a hedge of protection around your child and also staying up late to make sure they get home safe. Or driving safely while your children are in your car but not trusting their safety when others drive your kids around. The things we do not give to God are the things we do not trust He can handle. As it says in the word, we must go to Jesus for our protection and have that unseen faith that He will protect us and our loved ones as well (Psalms 11.1).

Like some of us I learned to lean on Jesus late in life. I gave my life to Jesus in my forties. The funny thing is I was led to baptism in my teens. I was sitting in church and that still small voice said, "come to me" and I got up and walked to the front of the church. Mind you this is the same church that was not feeding me, and asked to be baptized. Even though I was not being fed by the people in the church building, Jesus was in me. I, like many, played the world card and partied for a long time, BUT GOD! He never left me and He never forsake me. (Hebrews

13:5) Once I truly gave my life over to Jesus, I realized He not only kept me my entire life, He also answered my prayers. You never realize how much Jesus has always been in your life until you look back at your life or read your journals you may have kept and see all of the things Jesus had done in your life and troubles He has kept you from.

I thought I knew what I needed in my life so I led it that way; the way of my own understanding. Once I put my life in the hands of Jesus, I realized I was so wrong that it was not even funny. The more I started praying and thanking Him for His mercy and grace the moreand my life began to change for His and my good. It was 1998 when I began to pray for a man to come into my life who would be the kind of man like my dad. No, my prayers were not answered in my time, however they were answered in God's time. I started praying in January of 1998 and my husband came into my life in January of 1998. Boy is God a speedy God! One day as I stood watching the dolphins swim by on my fifteen-minute break at my job in Southern California. I turned and saw a man walking behind me. He turned and our eyes met and at that moment I heard that still small voice saying, "There is your husband". Of course, I was thinking, get thee behind me devil! Stop playing with my head. That's what we do. We hear His voice and think it cannot be Him. We say, He is not talking to me? He WAS talking to me and I was amazed that the creator of the universe was talking to little ol' me. As He would have it, in 2002 we were married and have been together under God ever since. (Joshua 24:24). When my husband and I got together we left California and moved to Nevada where we found a church together. There we learned to put Jesus in our lives more and how to grow our faith more with each coming day. This allowed for a stronger marriage and a better relationship not only with each other but with God.

My husband, being a veteran from the Marine Corps like many others, applied for disability due to the helicopter accidents endured and many other things that broke his body down over the years serving in the military. Like many, he was denied and put on the back burner. He had been fighting the government since he was discharged in 1984. Once we got together, we began to fight together with no luck, or so we thought. Jesus is always providing for us whether we know it or not. (Philippians 4:19). We really got involved in our church and lived life like Jesus was walking next to us. One Sunday the message was on tithing. It really radiated with us because we were tithing like a two-year-old who found a few pennies in the street each week. We gave offerings from whatever was in our pockets which was next to nothing. That message was for us that day in 2013. We began tithing ten percent with joy. It was not like pulling teeth but it filled us with happiness to give back to our God. (Deuteronomy 26). On the Sunday following the message, we made sure to tithe properly and when I tell you Jesus shall provide, Hallelujah, He did! The following weekend we received a retroactive check (back pay) from the Veterans Administration for my husband's disability of almost one hundred percent. God is so good. It is hard to put into words, just how good He is to the faithful. Testifying of His goodness is a form of praise to Him.

My husband who came from a fire and brimstone Baptist church in Arkansas and me, coming from a Baptist church in California did not stop the Lord our God from keeping us on the journey He had set for us both. Even though it was a difficult path, or so we thought, to get to where we are today; Jesus has always been there for us. Being raised in a life of partying and not knowing Jesus in our home life we still found our way to Him. We still have Hm in our lives daily from morning to night. He is our Savior. Once we obeyed and not only sacrificed, we were blessed and able to bless others as well. (John 15:10). We told our financial analyst at the time about our testimony of how God provided that financial blessing and she cried. It filled her with joy as well. We share our testimony every chance we get. He said spread the good news everywhere you go. (Acts 14:7).

Getting closer to Jesus was in fact the best thing to ever happen to me and my family. The testimonies that have come from getting closer to Him have been pure amazement. For those who do not believe, you do not know what you are missing. Some may believe their lives are perfect the way they are now; try my God and it would not only be the icing on the cake but it will be waking up to a joy you could never imagine. Some believe their blessings come from worldly things. God is the creator of all things and He is a jealous God. He is the one we go to for all things good and bad. (Genesis 2:4).

Even though I grew up in a household that did not really praise God audibly every day, I still know He guides our footsteps. Finding a husband and receiving the miracle of the approval of the Veterans Administration disability were just a few of the many testimonies I personally have. You may also have many testimonies that you do not even realize you have. We sometimes think it was just the luck of the draw. I know you have times in your life that made you think that way; however, Jesus is always with you guiding your footsteps and the blessings are always there (Psalms 119:133).

Having a praying grandmother is what gave some of my family members a foundation, God's foundation. Even though we each sinned throughout our lives, Jesus still forgave us for our sins by dying on the cross. (Colossians 1:20). We cannot go through life believing that our current sins will keep us from the love of Jesus. He died to save us from sin. He died so we could be dead to sin and healed (1 Peter 2:24). When we have troubles or situations, we believe we cannot handle we should turn to Jesus. Whether it is pain, road rage, marital problems or anger management we should first turn to Jesus. I was always angry or quick to anger growing up. I felt like people were disrespecting not only me but all individuals. I was not sure why I felt that way most of my life but I do know now. The Holy Spirit had a hold of me from the beginning. I knew wrong from right and I really did not like people doing wrong to others. Even though I was doing wrong in my own life, that was separate and something I needed to deal with inside of me. I wanted to look out for everyone else. I know that part was Jesus guiding me and the other part was my choice of following the worldly god. He gives us the amazing choice to either follow Him or follow the world. I finally chose Jesus and my life has been lifted to heights beyond belief for the non-believer (Ephesians 3:20). For true protection we must receive Jesus in our lives. If we go to Jesus first and foremost, we are better off than if we make choices from our own understanding (Proverbs 3:5). Being an angry young person made me just that, an angry person. When I started going to Jesus for all of my issues, the less issues came into my life. I began enjoying life more and putting all of my problems on the cross more and more. Back in the day I would go to the world in anger and nothing would be solved; it would just become another day of the same anger. I realized going to Jesus made for a better me. One day I was driving and a car pulled in front of me on the freeway and I got angry at the person. Even though I did not know that person I was angry all day. That did not change anything for that person, it only changed for me. Some days I would allow that anger to last for weeks and I would begin to daydream different scenarios with different outcomes. This is basically meditating on that situation and nothing changing in my life for the good. Once I received Jesus in my life, situations like that would still arise, however I would go to Jesus first. I would say, "What would Jesus do?" or "Jesus, what would you have me do?" Jesus would say, "just bless that person and move on". I tried it and in the beginning it was hard but like a muscle I exercised my choice and meditated on His word instead of meditating on the situation. My days got better over time and I treated others with kindness instead of hate. I find repaying evil with good not only makes me a happier person; it also allows others to receive more happiness in their day as well. Just like the smell of popcorn permeates a room so can joy. People gravitate to joy more than they do to anger and hate. So, starting my day with Jesus makes for a joy filled favored day for me and everyone I encounter.

I had to stop blaming my upbringing for my life today. My upbringing was a guide and it was in the past. We are to pray for forgiveness of others past transgressions as well as our own (Matthew 6:9). I had to stop making life difficult and just learned to **Keep It Simple Stupid**.

LAKISHA ROUSSEVE

Lakisha Rousseve is married to Maurice Rousseve Jr., together they lead ROC, INC a nonprofit community development organization geared toward empowering and enriching the community, visit www.builtontheroc.com for more information. Lakisha is also the owner of Banner Wear, LLC a brand whose motto is, "announce and proclaim the new you". Wear your statement, purpose and future and leave the old man, old nature behind. Visit www.bannerwear.com to see how to get a free t-shirt. By the grace of God Lakisha writes prophetic stories which God uses as roadmaps for believers to obtain the promises of God. The Apostle Paul states in *2 Timothy 4:7*, *"I have fought the good fight, I have finished the race, I have kept the faith"*. Some versions say *"I finished the course"* so for this reason have these writings been orchestrated by the Almighty to help you navigate and finish what you have been created for and to receive His blessings! Visit www.lakisharousseve.com for more prophetic writings that will thrust you into another dimension in God.

www.builtontheroc.com
www.bannerwear.com
www.lakisharousseve.com

CHAPTER 19

The Crossover: The War On Expanded Territory

The Crossover! Scripture tells us Jesus continually intercedes for us and through us. **Romans 8:34**
It is Christ who died, and furthermore is also risen, who is even at the right hand of God, who also makes intercession for us.

Moses who was born by the power of intercession became *the great deliverer,* the person God would use to deliver the people out of bondage. There were obstacles, barriers and trials but through it all God was there. Although the story seems to begin at the burning bush, in actuality the preparation really began when Moses was a child. He was a child raised to learn the culture. I remember the day I was saved and the culture shock that I experienced. God began to reteach me and how He said it was through a dream. I had a dream of my teeth falling out, I woke up and immediately felt my face for my teeth (LOL). I later learned it meant God was replacing worldly wisdom for true wisdom. *James 3:17, "But the wisdom that is from above is first pure, then peaceable, gentle, willing to yield, full of mercy and good fruits, without partiality and without hypocrisy"*. Scripture tells us it was wisdom that was with God in the building of this world. ***Proverbs 8:22-24,*** *"The Lord possessed me at the beginning of His way, before His works of old. I have been established from everlasting, from the beginning, before there was ever an earth. When there were no depths I was brought forth"*. Scripture also states Jesus grew in wisdom and stature **Luke 2:52,** *"And Jesus increased in wisdom and stature"*, painting a picture of what's needed in order to grow in Christ. Back to Moses, the Bible goes on to speak of some miraculous things that took place, God's promise is backed with protection. Moses was outnumbered in the natural world but spiritually he outnumbered them because he had the Creator of all backing him. **John 1:1,** *"In the beginning was the Word, and the Word was with God, and the Word was God"*.

Lean in and listen. The Bible says God told Moses what to do regarding the people and Moses interceded against what God said. **Proverbs 1:20-21,** *"Wisdom calls aloud outside; She raises her voice in the open squares. She cries out in the chief concourses, at the openings of the gates in the city"*. I will not force my words on you *verse 24 declares because I have called and you refused*. So God granted Moses's request and did not kill them but allowed them to die off. That dying off = time. Time of not seeing the promises of God manifest leads to frustration, wavering of faith (faint heart) etc., so that generations did not see because the leader did not follow the instructions of God. Although He was a friend of God, God started working behind the scenes raising Joshua.

A new generation who had little to no remembrance of the bondage (mindset), Joshua was taught by Moses. God also taught Joshua by having him watch. We learn from others' mistakes. God told Joshua to take strength and courage. This was very important. Not only did He tell him to take strength and courage but also to prepare the people (consecrate the people) for circumcision, which is a prerequisite for obtaining the promised land. Romans 2 talks about the mark that a believer carries (that is circumcision of the heart). It's a painful process but the long term results are beneficial. I remember a church I attended which God used as a training ground for developing leaders (which He has since placed in their assignments and callings), were instructed to do a foot washing service. During that service the leaders washed each other's feet. Amongst leadership, husbands and wives washed each other's feet. We repented to God and apologized for our immaturity towards each other. Some leaders weren't able to do so and some did. Pride was the reason. Pride will keep you from receiving the fullness of the promises of God. This day and many years later I see the repercussions of those that did not participate. Washing someone's feet is a very humbling process.

God also said to Joshua you have never walked this way before so stay close. In other words, **Psalm 37:23** (AMP) *The steps of a (good and righteous) man are directed and established by the LORD, and He delights in his way (and blesses his path).* Your next Is with God. **Psalm 32:8 (KJV)** *I will instruct you and teach you in the way you should go; I will guide you with My eye.* Remember this place is a place flowing with milk and honey "(opportunities and potential)". It is a land of Promise. How many times have you heard of doors of opportunities opening that lead to more and more and more and God says I keep pouring and pouring until the cup runs over. That overflow shows up in the community. *Psalm 18:11 The rich man's wealth is his strong city and Luke 19:17 because you were faithful in a very little, have authority over ten cities.* That overflow shows up in the "next" generation and the generations that follow. You are blessed to be a blessing. We see this with David and Samuel and even continuing to Jesus. The blessings "the word" continued through the generations in that bloodline. The intercession of the intercessor reached far. *Deuteronomy 5:9-10 (KJV) For I, the Lord your God, am a jealous God, visiting the iniquity of the fathers upon the children to the third and fourth generations of those who hate Me, but showing mercy to thousands, to those who love Me and keep My commandments.*

LISA ALLEN

> 66 NEVER GIVE UP, YOUR BEST IS YET TO COME ONLY BELIEVE. 99

CHAPTER 20

Never Give Up

The Bible declares in 3 John 1:2, Beloved I wish above all things that thou mayest prosper and be in health, even as thy soul prospereth.

Sometimes sickness will hinder you from walking in prosperity. I want to encourage you today that not even sickness can stop the hand of God on your life. I'm going to share my testimony on how God healed me from Lupus and Fibromyalgia.

I just could not see how I was going to obtain wealth and be prosperous in life. I was bound by these two diseases that man said there is no cure. For six years I never had a pain free day. I suffered longer because I could not fight past the pain. The spirit of infirmity had consumed me. I thought this was the way I was going to die.

A memory is a powerful thing. You see, God had to take me back to the very first time I received my diagnosis. I remember sitting in the waiting room of the doctor's office, when an old lady walked out the restroom humming as she passed by me and gave me a tract that read, *"this sickness is not unto death but for the glory of God, so that the son of God may be glorified by it"*.

It was at that moment I knew God was going to heal me. "Lisa, who are you"? I responded what do you mean God?

He said, " *You are a spirit that live in a body, and that's the real you. How can you have lupus or fibromyalgia because it can't touch you? It cannot attach to your Spirit. You see your thoughts are in your head, but if man cut your head open he would not be able to see them, and why, because you my dear are a spirit".*

That was a defining moment for me. It was then I realized I'm here for a purpose and I can't fulfill my purpose in this body of infirmities. We have kingdom authority over sickness, and even if you are sick you still have purpose and you can't give up.

God gave me specific instructions that I will share with you. He told me to eat the Word. That's the first thing I had to do and I offer the same to you. Look in the back of your Bible and on a sticky note write down every scripture on healing and place them around your house, in your mirrors and your car. Read them until they become a part of you. The Bible says in Romans 10:17 *"faith comes by hearing and hearing the word of God".* (Romans 10:17). Here are two of my favorite verses:

Jeremiah 33:6
> *"Behold I will bring it health and healing. I will heal them and reveal to them the abundance of peace and truth".*

Exodus 23:25
> *"And ye shall serve the Lord your God, and he shall bless thy bread and thy water, and I will take sickness away from the midst of thee".*

I found a good church that taught the Word and started my journey. I had sticky notes everywhere, even on the refrigerator. Keep in mind, you have an enemy who does not want you to walk in prosperity. There will be many faith challenges but you must NEVER GIVE UP. I suggest you get you a prayer squad, a group of prayer warriors that's going to stand in the gap, pray and believe with you for your healing. We know that when you start praying, the enemy will turn the heat up. Even if you get shaky in your faith, NEVER GIVE UP. I believe my healing was delayed because I would let the pain put pressure on my mouth (words) and I remember saying, "God I'm getting worse". I was not speaking life into my situation but was speaking opposite of what the word says. The Bible says in **Mark 11:24**, *"Therefore I say unto you what things you ask when you pray, believe that ye receive them, and ye shall have them"*. There is power in your confession so only say what God says about your sickness, don't say what you feel, because you will have what you say. Push through your symptoms and declare God's word.

That applies to every area in your life that needs healing. The word of God says He will never leave you or forsake you, **Hebrews 13:5**. God was right there with me all the time. I would turn the TV on and somebody would be talking about how God healed them from cancer. Sometimes one of my prayer warriors would call just to encourage me. I would go somewhere and see something about healing. God always knows what we need and when we need it. Be careful what you say about your situation and DO NOT talk with people about your healing if they don't walk in faith. People are going to think you are not in touch with reality but just like the pain is a reality, God's healing is also reality. It's a kingdom reality and you must be in the kingdom of

God to understand. Our God is so amazing. Spending time in worship is a vehicle by itself. I'm telling you worship with the Father will take you places. I began to notice I was going somewhere. My situation was changing. I started having some good days, then my good days started to outweigh my bad days. I was now making every bible study and every Sunday service.

One Wednesday night in bible study, I was in worship when I felt something move from the top of my head to the sole of my feet. I began to cry uncontrollably. Even right now I get overwhelmed and have to take a "praise break". Writing this takes me back to that overwhelming moment. Glory to God!

I still didn't understand what really happened, because it wasn't uncommon to get overwhelmed with the presence of God in my church. The next morning, I heard God so clearly tell me to wake up. It was early. You see, getting up early was rare, because I was taking a bag of meds and I never woke up until late. I opened my eyes, sat up on the side of the bed, and noticed I felt different. I felt light as a feather. I knew at that moment the diseases were no longer in my body. I jumped up and started smiling so hard. I ran through the house, fell to my knees, began to cry and shouting to the top of my voice. I begin to give God all of the praise and all of the glory. It's been four years this July that I received a full manifestation of my healing. I no longer take medicines. After three more trips to my rheumatologist, taking blood work, looking at my lab values since being off the medicine, my numbers are lining up perfectly, leaving them amazed at the miracle God had given me. Science doesn't understand it. I will never forget my doctor's response. She said it's as if the virus was never there. Glory to God! Now I'm living the grace life, walking in my calling, working in the hospice field where I'm always ministering and praying with people. Yes, getting paid to do what I love. Every one of my needs are met. When I tell you God is giving me double for my trouble, to God be the glory for the things He has done.

BISHOP CALLEB O. ORUKO

For further information concerning the above mentioned
literature, guidance and counseling contact:
Bishop Calleb O. Oruko
Word Power Church/Approved School of Ministry
P. O. Box 2255 -05100
Kakamega, Kenya
E-mail: seasonofgod@yahooo.com or Calleboruko93@gmail.com

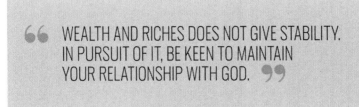

66 WEALTH AND RICHES DOES NOT GIVE STABILITY.
IN PURSUIT OF IT, BE KEEN TO MAINTAIN
YOUR RELATIONSHIP WITH GOD. 99

CHAPTER 21
God's Will and Concern

Holiness prepares people to manifest the life of God on earth while on the journey to eternal glory. Wealth is a tool for propelling God's work on earth. Money is a medium of exchange. Holiness without wealth can lead to frustration and shame. Wealth without Holiness is an abomination unto God and is equivalent to vanity. It is not just enough to be a poor wise man (Ecclesiastes 9:14-16). Being poor is not synonymous to being holy or being under a curse, it can as well show that a person is still in his days of 'humble beginnings'. Likewise, being rich is not equivalent to being holy. It takes wisdom to unveil God's mystery of entrusting man with wealth as well as keeping a mutual friendship of Holiness with Him. *"Wisdom is better than weapons of war, but one sinner destroys much good"* Ecclesiastes 9:18 (KJV). God is the source of all things; and our focus should not be deviated away from Him. With God all things are possible. Our joy should not be based on material things but on the fact that when we have a mutual relationship with God, we have nothing to lose, even when all seems to have been lost.

This book is intended to unlock your potential and open your understanding to the fact that it is possible to be holy and wealthy. Never limit wealth simply to movable and immovable properties; Think broad and wide as you deal with the concept of wealth. May this book be a manual to lead each reader into unfolding the hidden mystery of God's abundant riches in glory, kept for all His sons. Glory and gold goes hand in hand, especially when coupled with understanding and hard work.

Read this book with a clear motive, sincere heart and an open eye of understanding. Study it to be holy, believe it to be secure and, practice it to be rich. Holiness is achievable while riches are workable. Every good and perfect gift comes from the Lord who is no respecter of persons nor does He discriminate against anyone. Before reading further, I will treat this article with due honor as a gift; promise to study it keenly to the end so as to capture the inspiration and the revelation behind every statement. Prayerfully dedicate yourself to be holy in wealth and share the benefits of this book with others.

1. GOD'S WILL AND CONCERN

God is truly concerned about our financial and material prosperity just as He is concerned with our spiritual well-being.

2Peter 1:3-4 (KJV),
> *"According as His divine power hath given to us all things that pertain unto life and godliness, through the knowledge of Him who hath called us to glory and virtue: Hereby are given unto us exceeding great and precious promises that by these ye might be partakers of the divine nature having escaped the corruption that is in the world through lust"*

3John 2 (KJV),

> *"Beloved, I wish above all things that thou mayest prosper and be in good health even as your soul prospers".*

One's righteousness and possessions are interrelated. One's spiritual stability is sustained by his material welfare whereas his material productivity is propelled by his spirituality. It is wrong to equate poverty to righteousness; as a matter of fact, poverty in most cases leads to wickedness. Most poor men have wicked imaginations against others who seem to be better than they are. There is an increase of insecurity in many places due to the high rate of poverty. It is not good just to be a poor wise man; it is better to be wise and wealthy by God's grace. In Ecclesiastes 9:14-16 (NIV) The Bible states, *"There was once a small city with only a few people in it. And a powerful King came against it, surrounded it and built a huge siege works against it. Now there lived in that city a man poor but wise, and he saved the city by his wisdom. But nobody remembered that poor man. So I said, 'Wisdom is better than strength; but the poor man's wisdom is despised, and his words are no longer hidden."*

In these last days, the devil uses poverty as a tool to destroy the work of God like never before. Poverty leads to bitterness, shame, enmity and forgetfulness. Consider the following verses and begin fighting poverty just as sickness and sin:

Psalm 34:6 (NIV),

> *"This poor man called, and the Lord heard him, and saved him out of all his troubles."*

Proverb 14:20 (NIV),

> *"The poor are shunned even by their neighbors, but the rich have many friends."*

It is God's will for everyone who believes in Him to have full satisfaction and enjoyment. In <u>Ecclesiastes 3:11-13</u>, *"He hath made everything beautiful in his time: also He hath set the world in his heart, so that no man can find out the work that God maketh from the beginning to the end. I know that there is no good in them, but for a man to rejoice, and do good in his life. And also that every man should eat and drink, and enjoy the good of all his labor, it is the gift of God."*

Ecclesiastes 8:14-15 (NIV)

> *"There is something else meaningless that occurs on earth; righteous men who get what the wicked deserve, and wicked men who get what the righteous deserve. This too, I say, is meaningless. So I commend the enjoyment of life, because nothing is better for a man under the sun than to eat and drink and be glad. Then joy will accompany him on his work all the days of the life God has given him under the sun".*

However, the Bible warns against being overtaken by wealth, and states that wealth should be enjoyed and not worshiped; shared with others and accompanied by good works. Nothing competes with God for worship like material things, especially money.

1Timothy 6:17-18 (KJV)

> *"Charge them that are rich in this world, that they be not high-minded, nor trust in uncertain riches but in the living God, who giveth us richly all things to enjoy. That they do good, that they be rich in good works, ready to distribute, willing to communicate".*

Through Jesus Christ, we have a covenant with God to enjoy the blessings of God as promised to Abraham.

Genesis 12: 2–3 (KJV)
> *"And I will make you a great nation, and I will bless you, and make your name great; and you shall be a blessing. And I will bless them that bless you, and curse them that curse you; and in you shall all the families of the earth be blessed."*

Galatians 3: 6–7, 9 (KJV)
> *"Even as Abraham believed God, and it was counted to his righteousness. Know ye therefore that they which are of faith, the same are the children of Abraham. So then they which be of faith are blessed with faithful Abraham."*

Jesus came to deliver us from the curse of the law. In Galatians 3:13-14 (KJV) the Bible says, *"Christ hath redeemed us from the curse of the law, being made a curse for us. For it is written, cursed is everyone that hangeth on a tree: That the blessing of Abraham might come on the gentiles through Jesus Christ; that we might receive the promise of the Spirit by faith."* Poverty is part of the curse of the law (Deuteronomy 28:15-18)

Economic struggles came as a result of the fall of man. In Genesis 3:17-19 (KJV), God said to Adam, *"Because thou hast hearkened unto the voice of thy wife, and hast eaten the tree, of which I commanded thee, saying, thou shalt not eat of it: Cursed is the ground for thy sake; in sorrows shalt thou eat of it all the days of thy life. Thorns also and thistles shall it bring forth to thee; and thou shalt eat the herb of the field; in the sweat of thy face shalt thou eat bread, till thou return into the ground; for out of it wast thou taken: for dust thou art, and unto dust shalt thou return."* Before the fall of man, God made available all that man needed so as to enjoy life and have continuous fellowship with Him. It was His original plan for man to have dominion over all the earth, not just Eden, and be His steward over all that he had created (Genesis 1:26-28).

Through Jesus Christ, we are restored back to that original plan and are able to leave inheritance to our children's children". <u>Proverbs 13:22</u> (NIV) *"A good man leaves an inheritance for his children's children, but a sinner's wealth is stored up for the righteous."* As long as you are still living on this planet earth, you should invest as if you are living forever because your descendants' stability depends on your current efforts. You are free to pray as if you are dying the next minute but make sure you leave an inheritance behind for your descendants to enjoy.

Yes, it is possible for one to be holy and be rich at the same time. The God who makes us holy through Christ is the same God who owns everything. If He can respond to our cry for salvation, He can also satisfy our need for bread. Never allow your current situation to kill your morale; what you have acquired or achieved is not all that God has for you; much more is still in His storehouse waiting to be delivered at your disposal. Even if you have failed several times - maybe you are advanced in age; your background may disqualify you from being anything; you might have never known what a classroom looks like; but one thing is as certain as the dawning of the day, and that is, God is able to turn your life around. There is still a great chance of receiving wealth in abundance. With God you have nothing to lose.

God has made all the provisions for your wealth. He is really ready on His part; **ask**, **act**, **work** and **live** according to his set principles and you shall surely succeed in all your undertakings. Psalms 2:8 (KJV) says *"Ask of me and I shall give thee the heathen for thine inheritance; and the uttermost parts of the earth for thine possession".*

2. THE GOD –GIVEN WEALTH

In as much as God is the source of everything, not every wealth is God given; some is received through wicked ways, while some others are the devil's traps to capture one's heart and eventually destroy the whole person (John 10:10). Wealth gained through wicked ways leads to destruction.

Proverbs 15:4 (AMPV)
> *"In the house of the righteous is great treasure, but with the income of the wicked is trouble and vexation."*

God-given wealth will always bring the following:

a) Contentment

It is a state of being at ease and settled in one's heart with what he has. God-given riches will always satisfy one's needs and bring contentment in his heart with what he has. The opposite of contentment is greediness. Lust and idolatry thrives in an atmosphere of greediness. "But godliness with contentment is great gain" (1Timothy 6:5 KJV)

b) Confidence in Worship

One's economic status determines his spiritual stability. When lacking strikes, many tend to waver in faith. All things belong to

God and we are his stewards. As much as we get riches, we should not allow them to possess us. We should see riches as instruments and tools for worshiping our Creator. When one is settled in maternity, he can worship God wholeheartedly without murmuring. This does not mean that wealth propagates worship but that it contributes to being calm and focused in worship. Your economic well-being is a tool which the Lord uses to propagate His kingdom on earth.

c) Enjoyment

Every gift from God is perfect and is geared towards bringing enjoyment; just as we had noted earlier (Ecclesiastes 3:11-13). It is not godly for God's people to be frustrated by a lustful appetite for wealth. James 1:17 (KJV) states, *"Every good gift and every perfect gift is from above, and comes down from the Father of lights, with whom there is no variableness, neither shadow of turning."*

d) Distribution

God does not just bless you for your own sake, but also for the sake of meeting the needs of others. You should be a means through which other people's needs are met. Through our blessing, others get satisfied so that God's name is glorified. God told Abraham in Genesis 12:2-3, (NIV) "I will make you into a great nation and I will bless you: I will make your name great, and you will be a blessing. I will bless those who bless you and whoever curses you will curse; and all the people of the earth will be blessed through you". Other people were to be the beneficiaries of Abraham's blessings. Every blessing comes with a package that meets the needs of the church and other needy people. The needs of any given church are to be met by its very members. It is godly to assist others to acquire wealth.

1 Corinthians 10:24 (KJV)

> *"Let no man seek his own, but every man another's wealth."*

Philippians 2:3-4 (KJV)

> *"Let nothing be done through strife or vainglory; but in lowliness of mind let each esteem others better than themselves. Look not every man on his own things; but every man also on the things of others."*

e) Stability

Every believer in God has the potential to become materially stable in his own God-given capacity. Ephesians 1:3-4 (KJV) *"Blessed be the God and Father of our Lord Jesus Christ, who has blessed us with all spiritual blessings in heavenly places in Christ: According as he has chosen us in him before the foundation of the world, that we should be holy and without blame before him in love."* We are neither saved to starve nor redeemed to be reduced; but that we may be stable in all areas of life. *"Beloved, I wish above all things that thou mayest prosper and be in good health, even as thy soul prospereth"* 3 John 2 (KJV). It is God's will to supply all your needs according to his riches in glory by Christ Jesus so that you may be stable in your worship. Our stability and success depends on the measure of grace given to us by the Lord. Ephesians 4:7 (KJV) *"But to every one of us is given grace according to the measure of the gift of Christ."* We are not supposed to compare or compete with each other in wealth but to do our best to achieve all that is laid up for us.

Part of stability in wealth is that the future generations should be able to enjoy the fruits of our labor; A good man leaves inheritance to his children's children." Focus on giving a good foundation to your children so that they may be stable in their generation.

Psalms 112:1-3 (KJV) *"Praise be the Lord, blessed is the man that fears the Lord, that delights greatly in his commandments. His seed shall be mighty upon the earth: The generation of the upright shall be blessed. Wealth and riches shall be in his house: and his righteousness endures forever"* Wealth and riches does not give stability. In pursuit of it, be keen to maintain your relationship with God. Riches do not save in times of trouble and the wealth of the wicked is simply an investment kept for the righteous. (Psalms 49:6-11, Proverbs 13:22). The possession of wealth is not always a sign of God's favor. Jeremiah 12:1-2, Amos 2:6). Wealth acquired through corrupt deals and exploitation results in a curse to the possessor. In the New Testament, many warnings are given against letting money and things possess a person's heart. Jesus spoke of the treasures of the earth and in heaven and called upon his followers to be careful of which treasure they choose (Matthew 6:19-24,33). His parable such as the rich fool (Luke 16:19-31) strongly highlights the of putting one's trust in wealth . The only true and lasting wealth is the spiritual riches of God's grace (Mathew 13:44-46). Psalms 37:3-4 (KJV), *"Trust in the Lord and do good; so shall you dwell in the Lord, and verily you shall be fed. Delight yourself also in the Lord: and He shall give you the desires of your heart."* Psalms 37: 16 (KJV), *"A little that a righteous man has is better than the riches of many wicked."*

When riches increase, do not put your heart on them. <u>1 Samuel 2: 7–9 (KJV)</u>, *"The Lord makes poor, and makes rich: He brings low and lifts up. He raises up the poor out of the dust and lifts up the beggar from the dunghill, to set them among princes, and to make them inherit the throne of glory: for the pillars of the earth are the Lord's, and He has set the world upon them. He will keep the feet of His saints, and the wicked shall be silent in darkness; for by strength shall no man prevail."*

About the Author

PROPHETESS SHANIKA STEWART, VISIONARY AUTHOR

Prophetess Shanika Stewart serves in ministry with her husband Pastor Anthony T. Stewart who is the visionary of Active Faith Christian Center in Baton Rouge, Louisiana where they live to give and love to serve. Their vision and mission are to activate God's people's faith through His Word by preaching and teaching the Word of the True and Living God. Leading by example, they are so far from perfect, but serve a perfect God who is perfecting them daily. Prophetess Shanika Stewart is also the visionary of

Women of Faith and Hope (under the umbrella of Active Faith Christian Center) where she currently oversees "Thrive Becoming a Woman of Faith and Hope Movement. "

Prophetess Shanika Stewart love to outreach, she is a Missionary, a Prophet to the Nations, a Mouthpiece of God, and an Author of three books:

The Wounded Shall Recover
The Benefits of Your Release
From Poverty to The Promise Collaboration

Website: www.womenoffaithandhopethrive.com
Email: Womenoffaithandhope@mail.com
Email: shanikah5@icloud.com

Made in the USA
Columbia, SC
15 September 2022

67271969R00096